IMAGES
of America

DOWNTOWN
KINGSPORT

GREETINGS FROM KINGSPORT. This undated postcard showcases images of popular landmarks within the letters of Kingsport. Some of the images include Rotherwood, the Civic Auditorium, and Church Circle, all of which remain popular landmarks today. (Courtesy of the Archives of the City of Kingsport.)

ON THE COVER: Taken by local photographer David Peirce in 1958, this photograph shows the 100 block of Broad Street in Downtown Kingsport during the "You Auto Buy Now" campaign. Hundreds of cities across the country participated in the national effort to combat the declining sales of automobiles that year. (Courtesy of the Archives of the City of Kingsport.)

IMAGES
of America

DOWNTOWN
KINGSPORT

Brianne Wright

ARCADIA
PUBLISHING

Published by Arcadia Publishing
Charleston, South Carolina

Library of Congress Control Number: 2010941355

For all general information, please contact Arcadia Publishing:
Telephone 843-853-2070
Fax 843-853-0044
E-mail sales@arcadiapublishing.com
For customer service and orders:
Toll-Free 1-888-313-2665

Visit us on the Internet at www.arcadiapublishing.com

BIBLE CLASSES. Members of the Men's Bible Classes of Kingsport line the streets at Church Circle. This undated postcard shows the First Baptist Church (left) and the First Presbyterian Church (right). Church Circle became the focal point of the city's design with its distinctive spoke-and-wheel pattern that has become an iconic symbol of Kingsport. (Courtesy of the Archives of the City of Kingsport.)

CONTENTS

ACKNOWLEDGMENTS

The Archives of the City of Kingsport is fortunate to have a treasure trove of photographs and information documenting the history of Kingsport. First and foremost, thanks goes to all who have contributed and donated to the archives. Your contributions have made it possible to preserve and share Kingsport's unique history. All of the images in this book are courtesy of collections donated to the Archives of the City of Kingsport. A great deal of information in this book is research from the collections housed in the archives. As the archivist for the City of Kingsport, I am honored to be a part of the wonderful community that is dedicated to supporting Kingsport's history.

Much gratitude goes to members of the Friends of the Archives for their support, wisdom, and knowledge. I give a special thanks to all the board members, especially president Jolly Hill and treasurer George Hutchins for their time and input on this book. The author's royalties from the sale of this book will go to the Friends of the Archives. The Friends of the Archives contribute many volunteer hours for community outreach and programs, and the members are passionate supporters of our community history. The Friends of the Archives also provide financial support to the Archives of the City of Kingsport.

Thanks to Helen Whittaker and the rest of the staff at the Kingsport Public Library for their support and encouragement.

Another special thanks to Ned Irwin and Georgia Greer at the Archives of Appalachia at East Tennessee State University for their guidance and support, which has helped me get to where I am today.

Thanks to Elizabeth Bray from Arcadia Publishing for guiding me through the process of putting this book together.

Warmest thanks to my late mother, Teresa Johnson, who supported me in everything I did and whose love and guidance still shine on me.

Also, to my father, Jim Johnson, and brother Tony Johnson, thank you for your love, support, and encouragement.

I give an additional thanks to my husband, Mitch, for his advice, encouragement, help, and patience during the process of writing this book and in everything in life.

INTRODUCTION

Originally settled in the late 1700s, Kingsport's early history centered around its location on the Holston River and its use as a shipping port. Although it was once a fairly prosperous settlement, Kingsport began to decline after the Civil War and eventually was stripped of its original 1822 charter. As reliance on railroads throughout the region grew, Kingsport suffered because of its isolation from the railroad. The city was disorganized, and the growth of the area was dwindling. Kingsport, however, was fortunate enough to have a second chance at prosperity after its decline from the early days of success. That second chance came from the decision to include the city along the Clinchfield Railroad. This was advantageous for the "new" Kingsport and its reinvention into a flourishing, industrial city.

George L. Carter, most known for building the Clinchfield Railroad, was instrumental in bringing the railroad to town and laying the groundwork for modern Kingsport. Carter was also one of the first to envision a new industrial community at Kingsport. Facing financial concerns, Carter had to seek financial assistance and backers to complete the railroad. John B. Dennis, from New York, entered into the picture, becoming the financier of Kingsport in many ways. Dennis and J. Fred Johnson transformed the area, and together they spearheaded the development of modern Kingsport. A vibrant city came to life with the help of these men and their cooperative spirit.

Kingsport would not exist as it does today without the railroad. It brought industry, commerce, and growth to the city, which were all vital to the success of Kingsport. Industries located near the railroad were able to easily transport goods and materials as well as take advantage of the natural resources of the area. The railroad and the influx of commercial ventures were instrumental in recruiting a labor force and new residents. Kingsport's location on the railroad became a key element in the industrial activity that was fostered by Johnson. The railroad may have enticed industries to locate to Kingsport, but it was Johnson and other early leaders that encouraged the growth of the city. Johnson, who was described as the "one-man chamber of commerce," was a huge advocate for Kingsport. Not only did he bring commercial interests to the city, he also was influential in developing a sense of community pride that he called the "Kingsport Spirit"— something that is still evident today. Johnson and Dennis were relentless promoters of Kingsport. Although early leaders wanted the city to grow and flourish, they remained firm on not allowing Kingsport to become a boomtown. Kingsport grew fast, but from its inception, the leaders and planners of Kingsport accounted for long-term success. Chartered in 1917, Kingsport experienced rapid growth in its first few years, but part of what made it successful was in the planning of the city. Kingsport is unique in that it was laid out on paper before it became a reality.

The geography of Kingsport was rooted in the early city plans that were developed by John Nolen, the city planner. Nolen laid the groundwork for the "Model City," which was and still is Kingsport's nickname. The moniker derived from Kingsport's status as a planned city. Drawing on previous plans and the needs of the city, Nolen created a city plan with areas specifically zoned for industrial, commercial, spiritual, and residential growth and development. Nolen's ideas were centered on placing the industrial center along the river, houses at higher elevations, and commercial activity in between. Nolen's plan for the city also included businesses, schools, recreation areas, and parkways. An important feature of the city plan was the opportunity for growth and development throughout the years. Kingsport's history, although relatively young, is rich in commercial and cultural history.

At the heart of Kingsport's industrial and economic growth is the downtown district. Downtown Kingsport was at the center of the inception and growth of the city. As the hub of commercial and social activity, Downtown Kingsport had everything: shopping, restaurants, drugstores, grocery stores, movie theaters, automobile dealers, banks, and churches. Early housing developments and residential areas in Kingsport were strategically placed in close proximity to downtown, which allowed for easy access to the activity. People could walk to work, church, and stores. Downtown Kingsport eventually began to suffer due to the shift away from downtown to the suburban areas of the city. Wide-spread reliance and access to transportation allowed for people to move away from downtown and contributed to the regional sprawl of the area. It no longer became necessary or convenient to have Downtown Kingsport as the epicenter of the city. Kingsport has expanded its boundaries substantially since its early days, but downtown still remains an important facet.

Today, Downtown Kingsport is, like a lot of downtown districts across the country, undergoing exciting revitalization and redevelopment projects. Downtown Kingsport is in the middle of a renaissance with efforts to renovate buildings to their original facades, restore historical integrity, and bring activity back to downtown. New restaurants, bakeries, markets, and retail shops are opening, and there is, once again, dining, shopping, arts, and entertainment in Downtown Kingsport. The area is also home to the Academic Village, which is a center for workforce development and higher education. The Academic Village includes the Regional Center for Health Professions, the Regional Center for Advanced Manufacturing, and the Kingsport Center for Higher Education. The Academic Village has strengthened educational opportunities in Kingsport and aided in the redevelopment of downtown.

As exciting as it is to see Downtown Kingsport undergo this transformation, it is also important to remember it as it once was. All of the images in this book showcase Downtown Kingsport, starting in its infancy and continuing through its development into the late 1960s. This book is less of a comprehensive history of Kingsport and more of a celebration of the strong cultural heritage of downtown. As new life is being breathed into the area, it is important to remember Downtown Kingsport as seen in this book: a representation of the genesis of the City of Kingsport and what it has become today.

One

BUILDING THE
MODEL CITY

JANUARY 1916. This view of Downtown Kingsport was taken from Cement Hill a year before the city was incorporated. There were cow pastures, muddy roads, few businesses, and hardly any homes. The one thing the land did have was potential. Kingsport was carefully designed, and the layout of the city emphasized industrial, commercial, and residential zones while keeping in mind the future growth of the city.

MAIN AND SHELBY STREETS. This early image shows the intersection of Main and Shelby Streets. To the left in the image is Kingsport Stores, Inc., later called the Big Store. It was built around 1910. The building to the right is the Strand Theatre, which was the first movie theater in Kingsport. When the Strand Theatre moved to Broad Street, the building reopened as the Gem Theater. Today, the building houses the Downtown Kingsport Association.

MAIN AND BROAD STREETS. In this photograph, a crowd gathered at the intersection of Main and Broad Streets in front of the Kingsport Drug Store. The Kingsport Drug Store was located in the Tipton Building, which was built in 1915. The medical offices of Dr. E.W. Tipton and Dr. W.H. Reed were located on the second floor of the Tipton Building. Broad Street is also shown in this image during its early stages of development.

EARLY VIEWS FROM CEMENT HILL. These early views of downtown portray the old buildings of the Model City, which were based on the city plans designed by John Nolen. Both images were taken from Cement Hill. The above photograph was taken on February 22, 1917. The image shows the old Clinchfield Railroad depot (far right) that was later replaced with the station that stands today. The houses toward the right of the image were located on Cherokee Street. These houses were among the first residential developments in Kingsport. The houses were eventually torn down, and Cherokee Street became part of the downtown business district. In the photograph below, workers are busy carving out Broad Street toward Church Circle. Broad Street became the main thoroughfare of downtown.

PATRIOTIC RALLY. This 1917 photograph that was taken on Broad Street captures a scene from a patriotic rally centered on selling Liberty Bonds. Broad Street at this time was a dirt road. The building in the photograph housed the City Pressing Company, a dry-cleaning establishment.

A HERO'S WELCOME. A large crowd of Kingsporters gathered downtown on July 5, 1926. The crowd was there to see Sgt. Alvin C. York, one of the most decorated American soldiers in World War I. The event was organized by the American Legion, Hammond Post No. 3. J. Fred Johnson introduced York to the crowd, which was estimated at 20,000 attendees. The day was celebrated with a parade, music, and speeches.

PANORAMIC VIEW, 1924. This panoramic view of Downtown Kingsport was taken from the Clinchfield Railroad Station. The business district of Kingsport expanded to Main Street and Broad Street, ending near Church Circle. Early city planning included broad avenues, parkways, and ample greenways.

DOWNTOWN GATHERING, 1927. Only 10 years after incorporation, Kingsport was transformed into a thriving industrial town. This view down Broad Street shows a crowd gathered along the sidewalks and median. The landscaping around downtown was designed by Lola Anderson. Anderson, who arrived in Kingsport in 1919, was hired by the Kingsport Improvement Company as a landscape architect. A few years later, she married financier John B. Dennis.

KINGSPORT VISIONARIES. Pictured from left to right are Perley S. Wilcox, J. Fred Johnson, and John B. Dennis. Johnson and Dennis were considered the "fathers of Kingsport" since they were both early leaders and visionaries of Kingsport. Dennis financed and directed the building of the city, and Johnson carried out the city's plans. Both Dennis and Johnson were successful in bringing several industries to Kingsport, including the Tennessee Eastman Corporation. Wilcox served as director and general manager at the Tennessee Eastman Corporation, which was established in Kingsport in 1920.

KINGSPORT PLANS.
This 1916 letter,
sent to John B.
Dennis from J. Fred
Johnson, demonstrates
the interest and
enthusiasm Johnson
had for the City
of Kingsport.
Throughout his time
in Kingsport, Johnson
was instrumental
to instilling the
Kingsport Spirit
into the community.
Johnson devoted his
life to promoting
Kingsport. He
was known as the
"one-man chamber
of commerce."

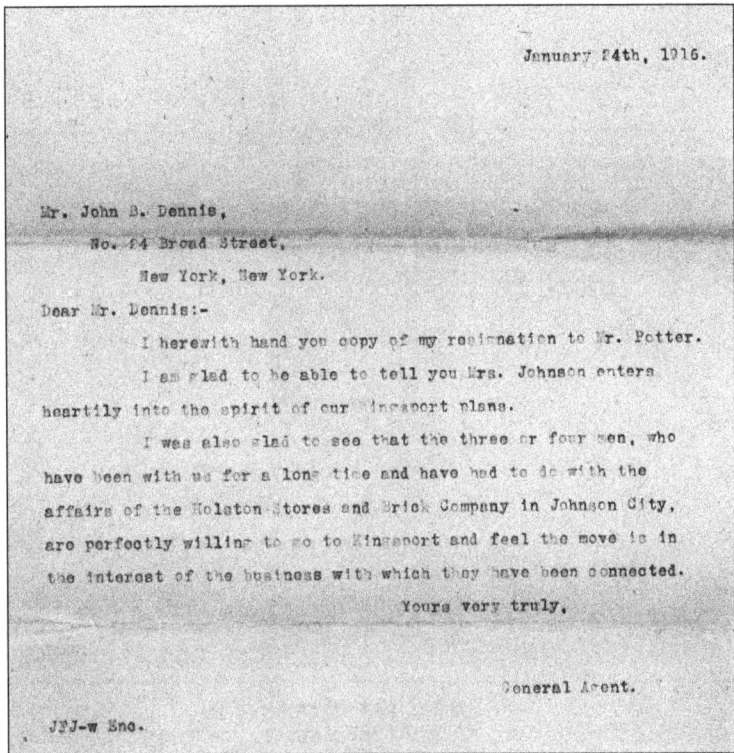

January 24th, 1916.

Mr. John B. Dennis,
    No. 44 Broad Street,
        New York, New York.
Dear Mr. Dennis:-
        I herewith hand you copy of my resignation to Mr. Potter.
        I am glad to be able to tell you Mrs. Johnson enters
heartily into the spirit of our Kingsport plans.
        I was also glad to see that the three or four men, who
have been with us for a long time and have had to do with the
affairs of the Holston Stores and Brick Company in Johnson City,
are perfectly willing to go to Kingsport and feel the move is in
the interest of the business with which they have been connected.
                            Yours very truly,

                            General Agent.

JFJ-w Enc.

KINGSPORT STORES. Kingsport Stores was first established along the Holston River as the Rotherwood Interstate Mercantile Company in 1906. The downtown store, built around 1910, was on the corner of Main and Shelby Streets. Called "the Big Store," it operated as a general store with a variety of departments that included hardware, dry goods, and groceries. In June 1923, the name was changed to J. Fred Johnson and Company.

US POST OFFICE. This undated image shows a group of people standing in front of the Kingsport branch of the US Post Office. At the time of this photograph, the post office was operated out of the Big Store, which was also known as the commissary. It was located on the corner of Main and Shelby Streets.

HOTEL KINGSPORT. The Hotel Kingsport, owned by H.O. Bunn, was located on Main Street. Advertised as a first-class hotel that was fire proof, sanitary, and modern, a guest could stay for a rate of $2 per night. In 1920, the hotel served as a temporary recruiting station for the military.

MAIN STREET POSTCARD. This undated postcard shows the Bank of Kingsport, Clinchfield Drug Company, and the Busy Bee Restaurant on Main Street. The Busy Bee was operated by Mickels and Gochs and was a popular restaurant in Kingsport. The Clinchfield Drug Company later moved to the Hicks building on Broad Street.

TIPTON BUILDING. The Tipton Building, built in 1915, was home to the Kingsport Drug Store. The Kingsport Restaurant, located next door on Main Street, was owned by Charles and Harry Mallis. The Mallis brothers closed the Kingsport Restaurant some time in the 1930s, when they moved to Broad Street and reopened as the Mallis Restaurant.

ELITE HOTEL. This image of the Elite Hotel (pronounced "e-light") was taken in February 1933. The Elite Hotel was located in the former Hotel Kingsport building. In 1932, the hotel was taken over by Nick Mallis. At one time, the city court was conducted in the basement of the Elite Hotel.

YMCA. This undated photograph shows the Kingsport YMCA at the corner of Center and Shelby Streets. The building housed a swimming pool, bowling alley, and gym. After the YMCA closed, the building was sold to the city and became city hall. In 1963, the building was demolished, and a new, modern city hall was built.

BROAD STREET CONSTRUCTION. Construction crews are seen in both photographs working on Broad Street. The 1938 photograph above was taken in front of Kingsport Drug Store and Shaffer's Lunch. Shaffer's Lunch was located at 112 Broad Street and was owned by James H. Shaffer. In the photograph below, construction crews work near the intersection of Market and Broad Streets. Other businesses in this image include Clinchfield Drug and Charles Store.

PUBLIC WORKS DEPARTMENT. As Downtown Kingsport was developed, cleanliness and sanitation became an important part of the Kingsport's image. In the photograph above, city workers pose with an early-model water tank and street flusher. In the photograph below, Roy Onks (left) and Frank Cloud (right) pose in front of the city's refuse-collection truck. Onks, known as the handyman of the public works department, came to Kingsport in 1924. As general foreman for the public works department, he oversaw the maintenance of city streets and waste collection. Cloud was the longest-serving city manager until his death in 1946. Kingsport was the first city within the state of Tennessee to adopt the council-manager form of government.

Corporate Limits, 1918.
Freda Covey poses at a speed-limit sign in Kingsport. The sign states that no loose livestock is allowed on the improved streets. The first paved streets in Kingsport were Cherokee and Main. In 1925, Covey married Dr. Charles G. Frye, a well-known optometrist. For more than 30 years, Frye had offices in the Tipton Building in downtown.

Kingsport Industries, 1925.
Kingsport was a planned industrial city. Although several industries were already in existence before incorporation, the railroad allowed for the development of modern Kingsport. J. Fred Johnson and John B. Dennis were successful in promoting Kingsport to new industries and encouraging the growth of the city. Industries located along the railroad were able to import and export raw materials, produce, and goods.

KINGSPORT INDUSTRIES, 1951. The Clinchfield Portland Cement Corporation, later known as the Pennsylvania-Dixie Cement Corporation, was the first industry established in Kingsport. The company began production in 1911. It was located on Hill Avenue at the foot of Shelby Street.

HOLLISTON MILLS, 1947. Holliston Mills of Tennessee, Inc., began operation in Kingsport in January 1926. The parent company, Holliston Mills, Inc., was headquartered in Norwood, Massachusetts. The plant, located along Reedy and Roller Streets and adjacent to the Kingsport Press, manufactured book cloth. Although the company shipped its product worldwide, one of the biggest consumers was the Kingsport Press.

KINGSPORT FOUNDRY, 1946. The Kingsport Foundry and Manufacturing Corporation was located on East Sullivan Street. The plant began operation in 1927 with William Ring as president. The foundry made iron, brass, and semi-steel castings. The plant was able to produce castings that weighed from less than one pound to 30,000 pounds.

THE PAPERMAKERS. In 1920, George Mead bought control of the Kingsport Pulp Corporation, which had been organized in 1916. Operating under the Mead Fibre Company, the plant manufactured pulp and paper. Roughly one-third of its product was purchased by the Kingsport Press. The company plant began producing white paper in 1923.

KINGSPORT PRESS. The Kingsport Press was one of the largest book manufacturers in the nation. Established in 1922, John B. Dennis served as chairman of the board. Production on the company's first order—50,000 copies of the New Testament—began on January 15, 1923. Louis Adams was the first president of the company. Col. Elbridge W. Palmer served as the company's second president for 29 years. The press produced textbooks, manuals, Bibles, novels, and collections of miniature books. The Kingsport Press had one of the nation's longest strikes. The strike lasted from March 11, 1963, until the spring of 1967. The Kingsport Press later operated as Arcata Graphics and Quebecor. The book-printing plant closed in 2006.

Two

CLINCHFIELD
RAILROAD STATION

RAILROAD STATION, 1920s. The Clinchfield Railroad was instrumental in the development of Kingsport. The completion of the Carolina, Clinchfield & Ohio Railway (CCO) in 1909 helped the city grow tremendously. The railroad attracted new business and a labor force, and its presence initiated the transport of materials in and out of the city. Placed on the National Register of Historic Places in 1973, the Clinchfield Railroad Station played a significant role in the growth of Kingsport.

TRAIN DEPOT, 1915. A group of unidentified men stand in front of the old train depot on Main Street. This photograph was taken on December 4, 1915. Posted on the building is the CCO bulletin that displayed the train schedule for the day. Prior to this depot, the first railroad offices were located in an old box car on Main Street.

Broad Street, Kingsport, Tenn.

VIEW DOWN BROAD STREET. This undated postcard shows a view down Broad Street toward the Clinchfield Railroad Station and Cement Hill. Cement Hill got its name because it used to serve as a burial ground for ash and kiln dust from the Pennsylvania-Dixie Cement Corporation. A dozen or more houses were built on Cement Hill in the 1920s. The last of the houses on Cement Hill were torn down in 1976.

CITY VIEW, 1928. Kingsport was once referred to as the Magic City because of its fast development and growth. It was said that it grew like magic. Buildings, houses, and churches were rapidly being constructed, and the population was booming. Downtown, as seen in this 1928 photograph, is anchored by the train station on one end and Church Circle on the other.

RAILWAY EXPRESS, 1951. The Clinchfield Railroad Station was designed by New York architect Clinton Mackenzie. Mackenzie, working with John Nolen, served as one of the principal architects of early Kingsport. Mackenzie was responsible for many designs throughout the city including the Kingsport Inn, Shelby Street Row Houses, and several neighborhood developments and homes.

Steam Engine. The man behind the railroad in Kingsport, George L. Carter, helped shape the area for regional commerce. It was Carter who brought in J. Fred Johnson, his brother-in-law, to work as an agent for the railroad. In financial peril, Carter had to turn to financiers from New York, like John B. Dennis, to complete the railroad. Dennis recruited Johnson to move to Kingsport and help develop and promote the city.

Railroad Employees, 1955. This photograph shows employees of the CCO railroad gathering for a group portrait. The portrait was taken during a company picnic. The group includes supervisors and other personnel.

ALL ABOARD. This image shows children from the nursery school of St. Paul's Episcopal Church preparing to board a train at the Clinchfield Railroad Station. The class was on a field trip in this 1950 photograph. The railroad in Kingsport provided a great deal of freight and passenger service.

SANTA TRAIN, 1948. A crowd gathers to welcome Santa Claus as he arrives in Kingsport aboard the Santa Train on November 26, 1948. The Santa Train started in 1943 as a goodwill gesture to rural residents in eastern Kentucky and southwest Virginia. The Merchants Bureau of Kingsport (which later became the Kingsport Chamber of Commerce) conceived the Santa Train as a way to entice rural residents to shop in Kingsport.

FREEDOM TRAIN. The Freedom Train rolled into the Clinchfield Railroad Station on October 1, 1948. The Freedom Train was an exhibit that toured the United States from 1947 to 1949, carrying 127 documents of historical significance. The documents included the Constitution, the Declaration of Independence, President Lincoln's Emancipation Proclamation, and the Gettysburg Address. The documents were carefully guarded by members of the US Marine Corps. People came from all over the region and waited in line for hours to view the items on the train. More than 11,000 people came to see the Freedom Train at its stop in Kingsport.

Three

CHURCH CIRCLE HISTORIC DISTRICT

AERIAL OF CHURCH CIRCLE. Church Circle is one of the best known landmarks in Kingsport. The iconic circle was a principal feature in the layout and design of downtown. This undated aerial photograph shows the four churches at the top of the semicircle, including the Kingsport Utilities building (left) and the Kingsport Inn (right). The Church Circle Historic District was placed on the National Register of Historic Places in 1973.

CHURCH CIRCLE, 1918. This early photograph of Church Circle shows the First Baptist Church on the left and First Presbyterian Church on the right. At the time this photograph was taken, the area was known as Civic Circle. Early city leaders and planners envisioned this area as the focal point of spiritual growth in the city.

CHURCH CIRCLE, 1929. This photograph of Church Circle was taken from the corner of the Kingsport Inn property in 1929. Pictured from left to right are the First Baptist Church, First Presbyterian Church, and Broad Street Methodist Church.

MOTHER DOBYNS, 1950. Lulu Lee Cooper Dobyns stands in front of the Red Feather thermometer in Church Circle. The thermometer measured the money raised in the Community Chest Drive. The Kingsport Community Chest was established in 1926. Affectionately known as "Mother Dobyns," she came to Kingsport in the early 1900s with her husband, James W. Dobyns, who became the first mayor of Kingsport in 1917.

CHRISTMAS TREE LIGHTING. The Christmas Tree Lighting event in Church Circle has become a community tradition. This undated image shows the crowd gathering to watch the lighting of the community tree. The event has been sponsored by the Downtown Kingsport Association since 1979.

FIRST BAPTIST CHURCH, 1961. The First Baptist Church held its first organizational meeting on January 14, 1917. The church's first building was built with funds that were provided by William Roller. As the congregation grew, the church building expanded in size. In 1927, a new building was erected around the original structure, and throughout the years, the church has continued to expand and build onto the structure.

SUNDAY SCHOOL. First Baptist Church set a record when 1,083 attendees met for a Sunday school class on January 17, 1932. All of them lined up to have their photograph taken for the occasion. Dr. Robert L. Wyatt was the pastor of First Baptist Church during this time.

BROAD STREET METHODIST CHURCH. Broad Street Methodist Church and the First Methodist Church both have ties to the Old Methodist Episcopal Church in the boatyard section of Kingsport. During the Civil War, the Methodists divided into Northern and Southern groups. The Southern Methodists organized their church on Church Circle as Broad Street Methodist Church. In the above photograph, taken in 1950, the church building is seen on Church Circle. The photograph below shows members of the men's Bible class gathering for a group portrait in 1958. Church members in this image are the Reverend E.E. Wiley (senior pastor), Flem Dobyns, George Taylor, John Wimberly, Dr. Broughton Hutchins, Charlie Palmer, Joe Young, Bill Boyer, Frank Dodson, Dr. William Wiley, and George Armour.

MENS BIBLE CLASS, BROAD ST. METHODIST CHURCH, REV. E.E. WILEY PASTOR 1958

First Methodist Church. The Northern Methodists organized their church, called the First Methodist Church, on Church Circle around the early 1920s. The church was built across the street from the Broad Street Methodist Church. The two churches existed side by side for several decades. In 1969, the two churches merged to form the First Broad Street United Methodist Church, and today, the church uses both buildings. Above, members of the First Methodist Church pose on the steps of the church in this undated photograph.

FIRST PRESBYTERIAN CHURCH, 1946. The First Presbyterian Church was organized at a meeting held in the home of the Hufford family in March 1917. The church was established with 52 members. The first services were held in revival tents and in an old theater on Broad Street. In 1918, the church moved into an old schoolhouse on the circle that was used until 1940, when construction on a new building was started on the same site. The building was designed by Allen Dryden Sr. The formal opening of the new church was held in December 1941. In the undated photograph below, children in the First Presbyterian Church's Sunday school class pose for a group portrait.

U. S. Post Office, Kingsport, Tenn.

400 BROAD STREET. This building on Broad Street was originally designed by Thomas Hastings, of New York, as the city's post office. The post office opened in this location in 1931. The post office later moved to Center Street, and this building became the location of the J. Fred Johnson Memorial Library in 1961. The building on the corner of Broad and New Streets still houses the Kingsport Public Library and archives today. Pictured below is a photograph of the library taken in 1962.

KINGSPORT UTILITIES, 1940. The Kingsport Utilities building, located on Church Circle, was constructed in 1932 and originally housed the Kingsport Power Company. The building shares some of the same architectural designs as the Kingsport Public Library, located next door. The building underwent a renovation several years ago and is now home of the Tri-Summit Bank.

KINGSPORT INN, 1960. The Kingsport Inn, located at 415 Broad Street, was designed by Clinton Mackenzie. The inn opened in 1917 and was the social center of Kingsport for several decades. The Kingsport Inn was closed after the last dinner was served on March 31, 1960. The building was demolished later that year.

APARTMENT HOUSES, ON SHELBY AND SULLIVAN STS., KINGSPORT, TENN.

SHELBY STREET. Included in the Church Circle Historic District are the row houses on Shelby Street, which were designed by Clinton Mackenzie. The Tudor-style apartment houses were built to house many employees from the Kingsport Improvement Company. The row houses were among the earliest residential developments in Kingsport. In the 1920s, rent was $30 per month. Today, many of the houses have been remodeled into shops and offices.

VIEW FROM THE INN, 1946. This photograph taken from the steps of the Kingsport Inn shows the post office (left), the row houses on Shelby Street (far middle), and the Kingsport Utilities building (right). The park in the middle of the image is now known as Glen Bruce Park. In 1968, the park was dedicated in honor of Glen Bruce, former mayor of Kingsport and active civic leader.

Four

MODEL CITY COMMERCE

WALLACE CRUM, 1946. Wallace Crum, owner of Wallace Fruit and News Stand, poses in the long-standing Kingsport institution. Mr. and Mrs. Wallace Crum began operating Wallace News in April 1941. The store sold magazines, paperback books, fruit, candy, snacks, and popcorn. The Crums retired in 1974 after 33 years in business. Wallace News is currently owned by Marty Mullins and is still located at 205 Broad Street.

KINGSPORT VARIETY STORE. The Kingsport Variety Store opened on Sullivan Street in 1915. The store was owned by J.M. Morton, E.M. Morton, and George T. Morton. The general store sold groceries, dry goods, and apparel. In this 1920 photograph, pictured from left to right are Charlie Ball, E.M. Morton, Wilbur Hammer, William Yates, and John Morton.

MERRY GARDEN. On August 22, 1927, the Merry Garden opened for business on Broad Street next to Farmers and Merchants Bank. The formal opening of the company was held in September and was attended by approximately 4,000 people. Under the proprietorship of J. Paul Warrick, the Merry Garden offered fountain drinks, sandwiches, tobacco, and other various sundries. In 1928, the company expanded to include prescription drugs.

FIVE POINTS SELF SERVICE STORE. Members of the Barnes and Bridwell families pose for a Christmas photograph inside the Five Points Self Service Store. The store opened for business on Charlemont Street around 1921. The store carried a full line of grocery staples and fresh meats. Given the self-service nature of the store, the store employed fewer clerks and advertised as a bargain center with reasonable prices. The shop also offered delivery service.

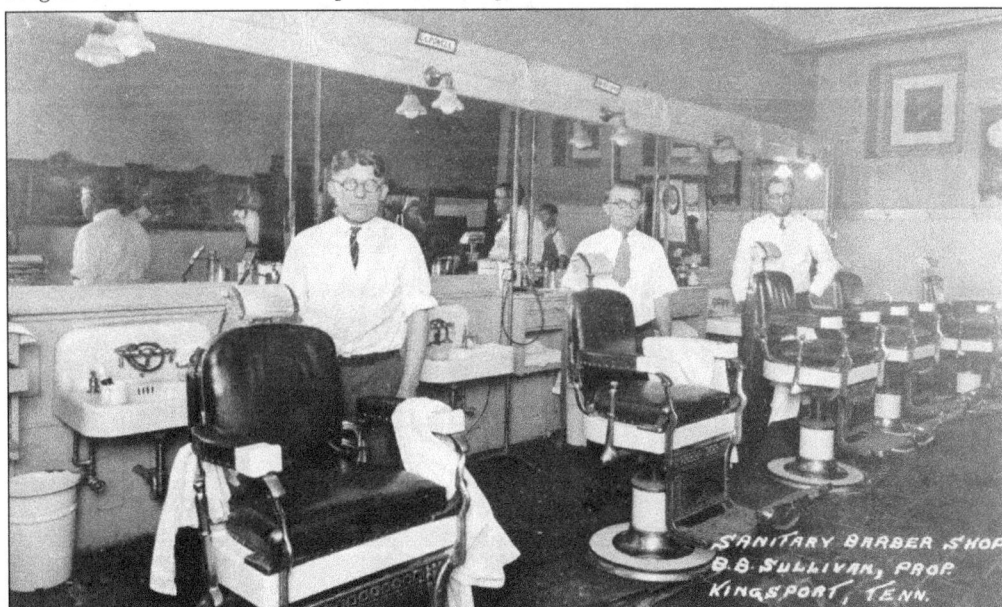

SANITARY BARBER SHOP, 1922. Sanitary Barber Shop, located on Broad Street, was owned and operated by B.B. Sullivan. Pictured from left to right are G.R. Walsh, L.L. Powell, and B.B. Sullivan. The shop opened in the summer of 1916. The first customer was H.C. Brooks. In 1919, the store advertised that a gentleman could get a hair cut for 40¢ and a shave for 20¢.

SOBEL'S. The Economy Store, which opened in 1925, was renamed Sobel's when the store was purchased by Morris Sobel in 1928. Sobel, with help from his brother Harry R. Sobel, successfully operated the popular store for decades. The brothers were both immigrants from Poland. The store became one of the finest in the region. Originally located at 130 Broad Street, Sobel's moved to 248 Broad Street for a time, then moved to its final location at 200 Center Street in 1948. In 1984, Norman and Hanne Sobel purchased the store from Morris Sobel, and they operated it until it closed in 2000. Sobel's was a pioneer business in Kingsport. Offering credit accounts to its customers in 1935, it became the first store in Kingsport to do so. Sobel's was also the first store in Kingsport to have a commercial website, which launched in 1995.

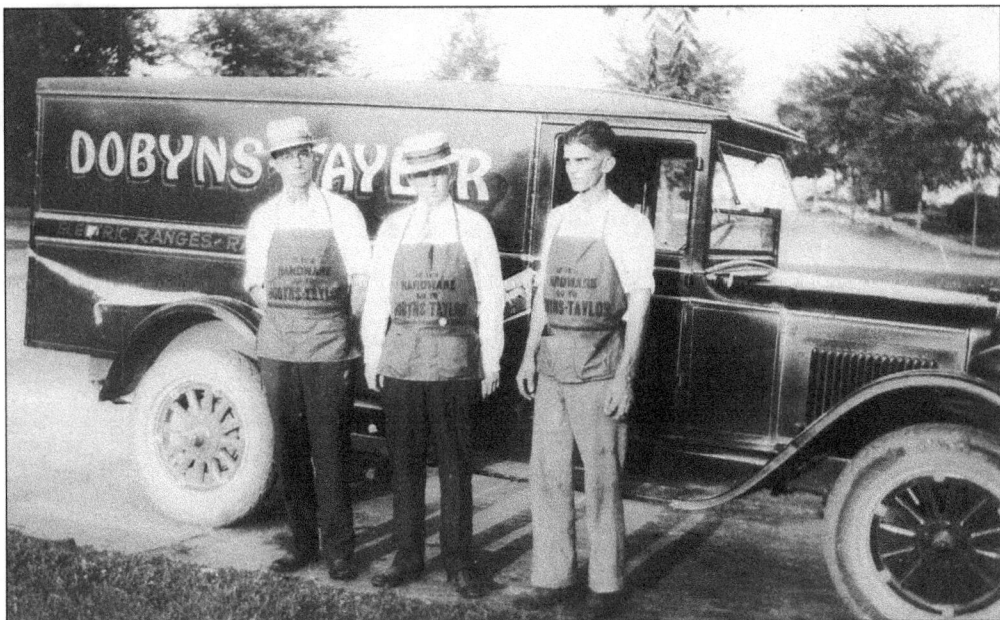

DOBYNS-TAYLOR.
Dobyns-Taylor
Hardware Company,
started by S. Flem
Dobyns and George W.
Taylor, was Sullivan
County's largest
hardware store for a
time. Established in
1922, the company
carried farm
machinery, cement,
paint, varnish, stoves,
ranges, glass, kitchen
furnishings, harnesses,
chinaware, jewelry, and
sporting goods. Above,
unidentified employees
pose for an undated
photograph in front
of a Dobyns-Taylor
delivery truck. At
right, D.A. Henderson
poses in front of a
display of seeds at the
store. The photograph
of Henderson was
taken in 1946.

ACORN DEPARTMENT STORE. The Acorn Department Store opened in 1928 and was located in the Roller Building on Broad Street. It sold a complete line of women's and men's clothing, shoes, millinery, and dry goods. H.M. Jones was the manager of the store. By 1938, the store had closed, and J. Fred Johnson and Company moved into the building.

HARKLEROAD FEED COMPANY, 1953. The Harkleroad Feed Company was owned by Margaret D. and Robert H. Harkleroad. The store sold feeds, seeds, insecticides, farm machinery, fertilizers, bee and poultry supplies, garden tools, and freezers. The store, located at 124 East Market Street, was known as the Checkerboard Store because its exterior was painted with a checkerboard pattern. Robert also taught classes to Victory Gardeners during World War II. The company was sold to Pratt's Farmland in 1956.

CITIZENS SUPPLY CORPORATION, 1946. The Citizens Supply Corporation was located on the corner of Main and Cherokee Streets and was incorporated on June 2, 1915. The business was founded by Charles E. Brooks. The company sold lumber, building materials, and supplies. Citizens Supply was instrumental in building Kingsport. The company furnished building materials for over 70 percent of the city's buildings and residences. The company motto was "If it's to build with we have it."

MUNROE'S, 1949. Ed Munroe adjusts a model television inside his shop located at 304 Cherokee Street. Soon after the television came to Kingsport in 1949, Munroe Radio Service changed its name to Munroe Radio and Television Service. Munroe and James Camp—who was the first person to own a television in Kingsport—converted a surplus Army ambulance into a television tester. They drove around the streets of Kingsport to determine where a signal could be reached.

CHARLES STORE, 1950. The Charles Store opened at the corner of Broad and Market Streets in April 1929. In 1950, the store had a significant renovation and expansion. One of the biggest additions was a marble clock tower on the facade. The grand reopening celebration was held in June. In the photograph below, the interior of the store is crowded with customers during the reopening.

SPORT SHOP, 1946. Kingsport's first exclusive sports store opened for business in 1945 at 111 East Market Street. The Sport Shop, owned by John R. Gouge and Harold Slagle, sold sporting goods, guns, ammunition, camping equipment, fishing supplies, hunting supplies, clothing, bicycles, and boats. The company's motto was "Everything for the sportsman."

W.B. GREENE COMPANY, 1952. Formally opened in November 1940, the W.B. Greene Company was located at 115 East Center Street. Owned by William Burton Greene, it was a popular store in Downtown Kingsport. The store sold hardware, appliances, electrical equipment, furniture, toys, clothing, and sporting goods. Pictured is an unidentified employee at a counter inside the store. Greene was active in the local business community for decades.

BETTY GAY, 1947. Betty Gay, located at 207 Broad Street, sold ladies' coats, suits, dresses, furs, accessories, and shoes. The store opened its doors in Kingsport in 1947, making it the 50th store opened by the chain of women's apparel stores. Betty Gay was a popular downtown store until 1976, when it moved out of downtown and into the Kingsport Mall on Eastman Road.

DARLING SHOP, 1947. The Darling Shop opened on Broad Street in the old Cincinnati Bargain Store building in 1932. The store was advertised as a women's ready-to-wear shop and was described as being distinctly feminine. This photograph of employees from the Darling Shop was taken in 1947, around the time the store was remodeled.

DIANA SHOPS, 1959. Diana Shops, a dress store chain, opened in Kingsport in 1949 next to McCrory's on Broad Street. In November 1959, the company moved to the newly constructed building at 230 Broad Street. The shop was located between S.H. Kress and Fuller & Hillman. Below, employees pose inside the store's new location. Diana Shops carried a complete line of dresses, coats, suits, sportswear, beachwear, and lingerie. The store was managed by Shirley Wright.

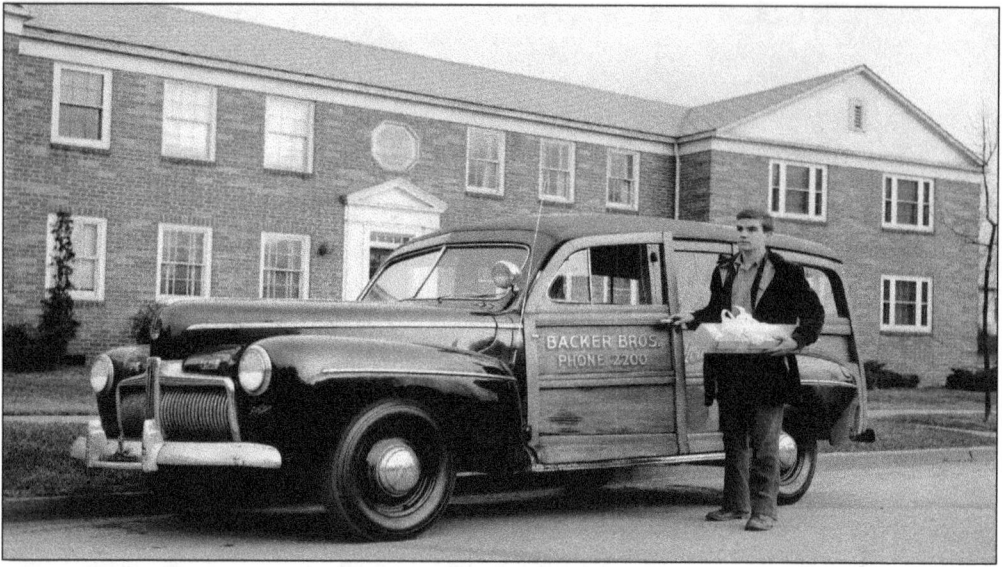

BACKER BROTHERS, 1946. This image shows an unidentified employee of Backer Bros. Flowers posed in front of the company's delivery vehicle. The image was taken in front of the Herndon Apartments on the corner of Watauga Street and Charlemont Avenue. Backer Bros. Flowers was owned by D.W. "Watt" Backer and Steve Backer. The store opened in 1941 and was located at 201 East Charlemont Avenue.

GODWIN HARDWARE, 1950. Godwin Hardware and Supplies was owned by Jesse A. Godwin. The company opened in September 1946 at 122 East Market Street, between Harkleroad Feed Company and Weaver's Shoe Shop. Godwin, a successful businessman, served as vice mayor of Kingsport from 1959 to 1961 and later became the city property assessor.

J. Fred Johnson and Company, 1954. This photograph shows an employee of J. Fred Johnson and Company assisting a customer in the hosiery department. In 1923, the company was organized to take ownership of the Kingsport Stores. As successor of the Kingsport Stores, the company was, at one time, the largest department store in East Tennessee.

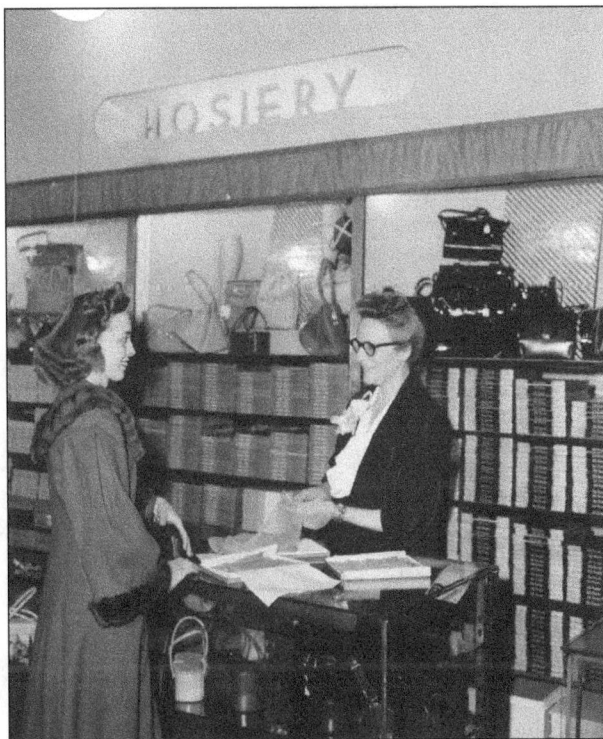

United Furniture Company. United Furniture Company opened on Market Street in 1935. Souvenir cigarette and cigar lighters were given out to customers on opening day. When this 1965 photograph was taken, the store was located at 143 Broad Street. In May 1965, the name was changed to Ball Brothers Furniture.

KINGSPORT CAMERA SHOP, 1950. The Kingsport Camera Shop was owned by Roy and Virginia Poe. The shop was located on Cherokee Street. Services included camera repair, photography equipment, photofinishing, and new and used camera sales. Virginia Poe was a graduate of the Kodak Sales Training School for Kodak dealers in Rochester, New York. Some time in the late 1960s, the shop was purchased by David Walsh and Jim Wells.

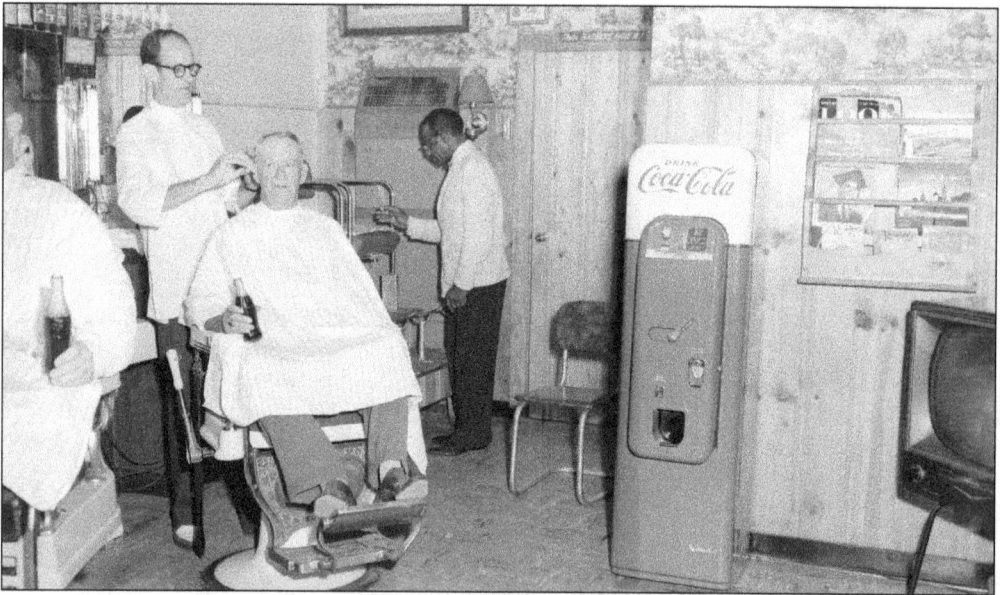

MACANACK BARBER SHOP. The Macanack Barber Shop was located at 504 East Center Street. This 1957 photograph shows barber Mac Jones cutting a client's hair. The barbershop was owned by Mack "Mac" Jones and Axley "Ack" Burdine. The name of the establishment came from combining the nicknames of the two owners.

WINN'S, 1964. Winn's Cut Rate was located at 122 East Market, next door to Kyker-Hodge Furniture. The shop sold sporting goods, army surplus, and jewelry. Winn's went out of business in 1974. It was owned by David Silber.

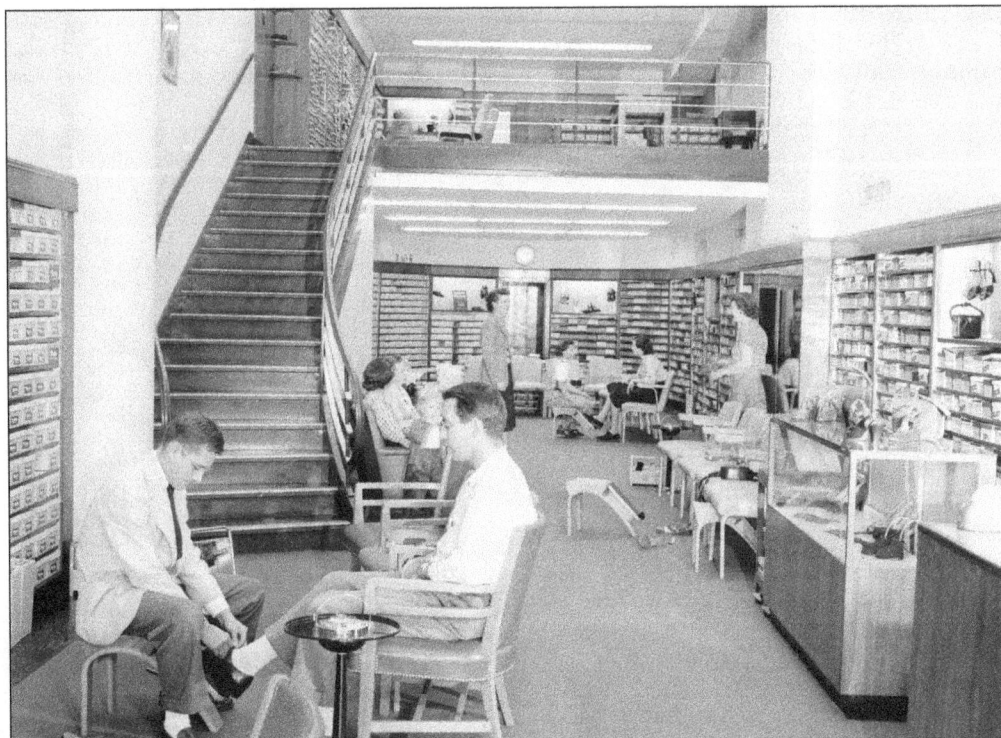

HARRISON'S BOOTERY, 1950. Harrison's Bootery was located at 206 East Center Street. It was owned by John W. Harrison Jr., who also owned Harrison's Shoe Store on Broad Street.

JEWEL BOX, 1953. In 1922, Harry Lipman opened the first Jewel Box in Greensboro, North Carolina. The Kingsport store opened on October 28, 1937. The store, located at 134 Broad Street, carried jewelry, diamonds, silverware, luggage, gifts, glass, and chinaware. The Jewel Box was owned by Nedd W. Cohen and Henry Lipman.

JORDEN'S JEWELERS, 1946. This photograph of Jorden's Jewelers was taken inside the store located at 149 Broad Street. Jorden's Jewelers was owned by Adolf Lipman.

KINGSPORT JEWELRY COMPANY, 1947. This photograph shows customers of the Kingsport Jewelry Company lining up outside the store for the $1 Grab Box Day. The Kingsport Jewelry Company was located at 113 Broad Street.

JOSEPH'S. In 1940, Joseph's Loan Office, owned by Joseph Heller, moved from Market Street to this location at 115 Broad Street. The store was previously named the Kingsport Barter Exchange and was established in 1933. It was later renamed Joseph's Music Center, and the store reportedly sold Maybelle Carter her first Autoharp. Heller was instrumental in forming the Kingsport Symphony Orchestra and the Kingsport Community Band.

HUTCH-WALLIN FLORIST, 1946. Hutch-Wallin Florist was located at 105 East Main Street. Formerly named the Magic City Floral Gardens, the shop was owned by Dr. Will Hutchins. His daughter, Ruth Hutchins Williams, is seen here in front of the display coolers inside the shop. The name of the business was derived from the boyhood nickname of Hutchins, "Hutch," and his wife's maiden name, Wallin.

BENNETT AND EDWARDS. This 1955 photograph shows two employees from the Bennett and Edwards Insurance Agency celebrating opening-day ceremonies at the company's new location at 214 Commerce Street. The company moved from its long-standing location in the First National Bank Building. It was formed by Carnot Jones Bennett and C.P. Edwards Jr. in 1916.

FIRST NATIONAL BANK, 1946. Customers are taking care of their banking business in this 1946 photograph taken inside First National Bank. Located on the corner of Broad and Center Streets, First National Bank was chartered on April 28, 1916, with William Roller as president. On November 9, 1931, the bank took over the operations of the Bank of Kingsport. First National was the first bank in Kingsport to open a drive-in branch.

SAVINGS AND LOAN, 1962. James Edwards (second row, center) poses with employees of the Kingsport Federal Savings and Loan Association, where he served as the executive vice president and secretary. Edwards was also the president of the Kingsport Chamber of Commerce in the early 1960s. C.P. Edwards Jr. was the president of the banking institution.

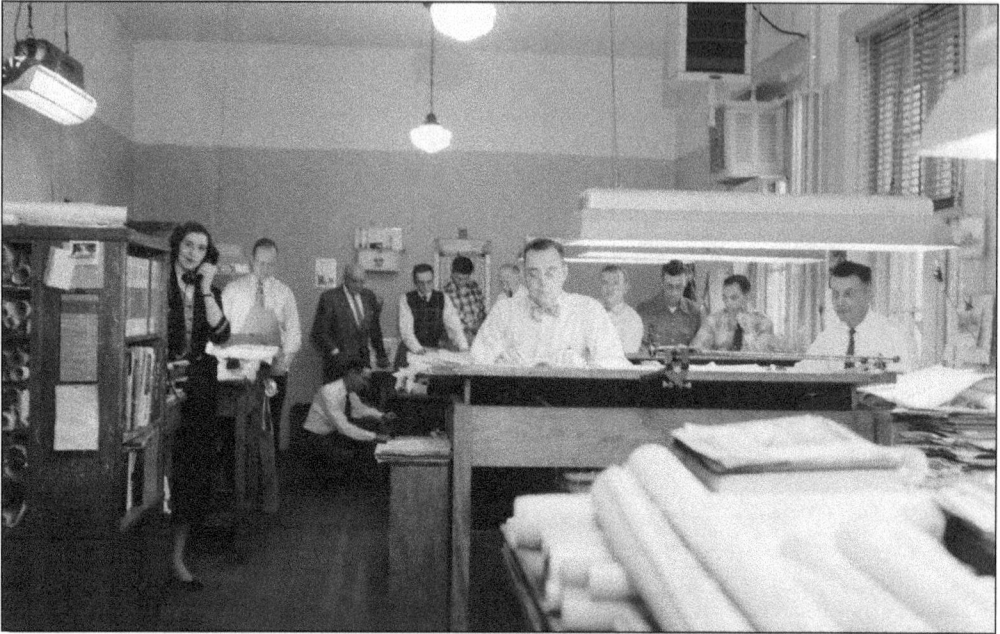

ALLEN DRYDEN'S OFFICE, 1955. Employees of the Allen Dryden Sr. Architectural Firm are shown inside the office that was located in the Improvement Building on West Market Street. Dryden established the first architectural firm in Kingsport in 1920. The first house Dryden built in Kingsport was the Shivell Home, located at 1717 Orchard Court. Today, the firm is operated by Allen Dryden Jr.

KINGSPORT TIMES-NEWS, 1946. The *Kingsport Times* was first published as a weekly newspaper in April 1916. Maj. Cy H. Lyle, R.D. Kinkead, and T.L. Anderson—all formerly associated with the *Johnson City Comet*—initially printed the paper in Johnson City and shipped the papers to Kingsport via the Clinchfield Railroad. Daily publication of the paper started in 1924, and in 1942, the *Kingsport News*, a morning edition of the paper, was started.

Five

MOVIE THEATERS

MOVIEGOERS, 1922. This photograph shows Ann Booher (right) and other moviegoers standing outside the Strand Theatre at 138 West Main Street. The Strand, opened in 1916, was the first movie theater in Kingsport. After the Strand moved to Broad Street, the building became home to the Gem Theater. The Gem opened on November 8, 1924, under the management of Don Williamson. The building was built in 1915.

THE QUEEN AND THE GAIETY. Hundreds of people gather on Broad Street in front of the Queen Theatre during a patriotic rally in 1917. The Queen was the second theater that opened in Kingsport. Located on Broad Street, it opened in 1917. By 1918, the theater was renamed the Gaiety. Pictured below is the Gaiety in 1918. For many years, the Gaiety was the site of Sunday worship services for the Kingsport Methodist Episcopal Church. By 1925, the Gaiety Theatre was closed, and the building was remodeled to house the Kingsport Office Supply Company.

CENTER THEATER, 1950. The Center Theater, located on Commerce Street, opened on January 26, 1948. Its first movie was *Magic Town*, starring James Stewart and Jane Wyman. The theater was operated by Tennessee Amusement Company president Jimmy Pepper, vice president Val Edwards, and secretary John Wimberly, who was also the company's treasurer. The theater was home to the Buddy Club, which was organized in 1948. Meetings were held on Saturday mornings, and the club had a membership of more than 2,000 children.

RIALTO. The Rialto was located at 400 Cherokee Street in Five Points. The theater opened in 1921. The movie showing at the Rialto in this 1951 photograph was *Show Boat*, starring Howard Keel and Ava Gardner. The theater closed around 1961.

STRAND THEATRE. The Strand Theatre was the first movie theater in Kingsport. Originally located on the corner of Main and Shelby Streets, it moved to 140 Broad Street (the former home of Goodwin Furniture Company) around 1925. The Strand burned down on December 22, 1945. The fire was discovered in the balcony just in time to usher nearly 800 patrons out of the building. There were no injuries, but the theater was destroyed. It was rebuilt, and the Strand reopened in 1947. The Strand officially closed on October 23, 1982. In 1989, the Restoration Church moved into the historical theater building. Above, this 1948 photograph shows the exterior of the Strand. In the undated photograph below, an unidentified employee is working at the Sweet Shop inside the Strand.

MOVIES AT THE STRAND. Both of these photographs, taken in 1940, were captured during an unknown children's event at the Strand Theatre. The theater was the host to a variety of events, including a children's movie club. The theater also hosted performances of the Kiwanis Kapers, a local variety program. In July 1939, Gene Autry, "the Singing Cowboy," appeared at the Strand. The first services of the First Christian Church were held at the Strand when the theater was located in its original location on Main Street.

STATE THEATRE, 1939. The State Theatre was located at 155 Broad Street and opened on March 6, 1936. Its first movie was Bing Crosby's *Anything Goes*. The majority of building supplies for the new venue were furnished by Citizens Supply Corporation. The interior of the State Theatre was designed by Italian artist Navino Nataloni. Nataloni, employed by the Wil-Kin Theatre Supply Corporation, was a leading interior decorator of movie theaters around the country.

GONE WITH THE WIND, 1940. The American classic *Gone with the Wind* premiered in Kingsport at the State Theatre on February 26, 1940. The Tennessee premiere was a huge event with hundreds of moviegoers in attendance.

POPEYE CLUB. The Popeye Club at the State Theatre was organized by Jimmy Pepper, the manager of the theater. The first meeting was held on May 9, 1936. Norma Faye Scott opened the meeting with the club theme song, "I'm Popeye the Sailor Man." Members of the Popeye Club met on Saturdays at 10 a.m. to watch movies and cartoons and participate in contests, giveaways, and other activities.

TICKET BOOTH. This 1950 photograph shows an employee of the State Theatre sitting in a ticket booth. At the time, admission for adults was 44¢. Children age 12 and younger paid 9¢ for admittance. The State Theatre closed its doors on March 26, 1978. However, the ticket booth still sits in front of the theater, which has been undergoing renovations to preserve its historical features.

Six

Drug Stores, Grocery Stores, and Restaurants

Kingsport Drug Store. The Kingsport Drug Store, built in 1915, was located on the corner of Main and Shelby Streets in the Tipton Building. Next door to the drugstore was the Kingsport Fruit and News on Broad Street. The Kingsport Fruit and News was owned by George W. Earles and J.C. Zarnes, and it opened for business around 1925. This 1946 photograph shows the intersection of Main and Broad Streets.

CLINCHFIELD DRUG COMPANY. Established around 1916, the Clinchfield Drug Company was advertised as "the place where quality and service meet." The company first opened on the corner of Sullivan and Shelby Streets but moved to Main Street in 1919. In 1923, the company moved once again, to Broad Street. This undated photograph shows Dr. Victor Boyd Freels (left) and unidentified men posing in front of the business.

LUNCHEONETTE. This scene from an undated photograph shows a crowd of patrons inside the Clinchfield Drug Company, which was among the pioneering businesses in Kingsport. When the company first opened, it was managed by R.I.C. Hawley. It was later managed by Dr. Victor Boyd Freels.

CLINCHFIELD DRUG, 1927. Clinchfield Drug moved into the Hicks Building on the corner of Broad and Market Streets in 1923. This 1927 photograph shows the business located at 160 Broad Street. The Hicks Building served as Kingsport's second hospital and was opened as a result of the flu epidemic in 1918.

FREELS DRUG STORE. Freels, founded by Dr. Victor Boyd Freels, formally opened its doors in April 1935. The store was located on the corner of Broad and Center Streets. Freels came to Kingsport in 1917 and was associated with the Clinchfield Drug Company for many years. Above, Freels was located next door to Sobel's in this 1946 photograph. At left, Dr. Harry Adams, a longtime employee of Freels Drug Store, poses next to a display for Alka-Seltzer in 1953. Adams started as an assistant manager when the store opened in 1935 and later became the manager and pharmacist of the company. He received his degree in pharmacy from the Medical College of Virginia in 1927.

HOLSTON DRUGS, 1950. Holston Drugs first opened in 1925 on Main Street. The company was owned by Harry Nelms, Dr. G.C. Lyons, and Dr. W.C. Lyons. In 1940, the drugstore moved to Center Street into a new building that also housed the W.B. Greene Company. The building was completed with an estimated cost of $90,000. Paul "Monk" Warrick was once the manager of the fountain and sundries departments.

COLE'S DRUG STORE. This 1953 photograph shows the exterior of Cole's Drug Store, which was located on West Sullivan Street next door to the Little Store. Cole's also had a location on Broad Street. The location on West Sullivan Street opened in December 1953. Cole's Drug Store was founded by Bob Cole from Knoxville. The store was managed by Leaman Holliman. Lotus Brandon was in charge of the soda fountain and lunch counter.

EARLES DRUG STORE, 1946. Earles Drug Store, seen in this 1946 photograph, was owned by Dr. George W. Earles. The store opened in July 1941 at 120 East Center Street. The building, owned by Earles and Dr. J.A. Flora, featured soda and luncheonette services in the drugstore on the first floor. The second floor was built to house a number of medical offices. Earles had previously been affiliated with both the Kingsport and Holston Drug Companies. He was assisted by Dr. R.C. Badgett, a licensed pharmacist. When Earles died in 1953, his widow, Janie Earles, along with sons George and Howard, continued to run the business. Janie was active in politics and organized the first Republican women's group in Sullivan County. She ran, unsuccessfully, for state senator in 1968.

EARLES. In 1960, Earles Drug Store moved a few blocks down from its original location to the corner of Center and Shelby Streets. The new three-story building featured Kingsport's first prescription drive-in window. The first floor housed the drugstore, cafeteria, and luncheonette. The second and third floors housed a variety of offices. Above, this 1962 photograph shows the new Earles, which was located behind J. Fred Johnson and Company. Below, this 1960 photograph, taken shortly after the new building opened, showcases the interior of the building. The store carried a complete cosmetic and sundries department along with the prescription center.

MARKET STREET GROCERY, 1933. In 1923, the Market Street Grocery opened in the former J.W. Johnson Grocery Store building on Market Street. C.B. Fleenor, manager of the J.W. Johnson Grocery, and Paul Bailey purchased the store from J.W. Johnson.

DIXIE MAID BAKERY, 1946. The Dixie Maid Bakery was owned by Lee R. Drury and Denzil S. Sample. The company sold retail and wholesale baked goods. Drury, seen in this image, poses with a cake made for the 100th birthday celebration of Gen. Julius Franklin Howell. Howell was the former commander in chief of the United Confederate Veterans. Dixie Maid Bakery was located at 200 Cherokee Street.

LET'S GO KROGERING. These 1946 photographs show the exterior of the Kroger Grocery and Bakery Company, which was located at 324 Cherokee Street on the corner of New Street. The Cherokee Building was located across the street from the Union Bus Terminal. In the photograph below, shoppers stock up on groceries and supplies.

A&P SUPERMARKET, 1946. The A&P Supermarket was located at 201 East New Street. This view of the store was taken from the side of the building on Commerce Street. At the time this photograph was taken, the store was managed by George W. Stott. The supermarket was affiliated with the Great Atlantic & Pacific Tea Company. The company was the first national supermarket chain in the United States.

MACGIL RESTAURANT, 1946. The Macgil Restaurant, opened on February 1, 1946, was owned by Joseph E. Gill and Felix G. McMillion. McMillon and Gill operated the restaurant in Maryville before coming to Kingsport. Gill retired shortly after the restaurant opened, and William F. Crain bought Gill's interest in the restaurant, becoming partners with McMillion. The restaurant was located at 209 East New Street.

PIGGLY WIGGLY, 1946. The Piggly Wiggly Store opened in Kingsport in 1939. The store was purchased by Ronald D. Liggan in 1941. Liggan served as the owner and manager of the franchise, which was located at 121 West Market Street. Next door was the Johnson-Gentry Furniture Company, operated by James M. Johnson and R. Calvin Gentry. The company sold furniture, appliances, radios, and electrical appliances.

GIANT SUPERMARKET. Giant Supermarket operated several stores in Kingsport and the surrounding areas. The store in this 1961 photograph was located on West Sullivan Street on Supermarket Row. Giant was locally owned and operated by the LaGuardia family. The company, founded by Thomas LaGuardia Sr., was called the Cut-Rate Market in the 1930s. The Royal Laundry and Dry Cleaning Company, owned by J. Fred Fauzie, had a branch location inside Giant.

OAKWOOD MARKET, 1956. Oakwood Market was another successful, locally owned grocery store. The first Oakwood Market opened on Eastman Road in 1947. In 1950, owners Wallace Boyd and James A. Stout opened a second location on West Sullivan Street. Oakwood was the first self-service grocery store in Kingsport and the first store to occupy what would become Supermarket Row.

MCANINCH FRUIT AND NEWS. This undated photograph shows the McAninch Fruit and News. McAninch Market was located at 702–704 Bristol Highway, which is now East Center Street. The business was owned by R.C. McAninch. Throughout the years, the McAninch family members were successful Kingsport entrepreneurs. The family also owned the Model City Motel, the Garden Basket, and McAninch Apartments.

LITTLE STORE. The Little Store was founded by Carl Young in 1930. Young followed in the footsteps of his father, F.W. Young, who was a successful grocer in Johnson City. The Kingsport store was opened for business in 1934. Carl Young's brother Kermit entered into the business at that time. Kermit Young operated the Little Store in Kingsport for several decades. The Little Store, which started in a 20-foot-by-35-foot storefront in Bristol, continued to grow into a very popular and successful company with locations throughout the Tri-City region.

SUPERMARKET ROW, 1954. After the Oakwood Market opened on West Sullivan Street, other grocery stores began to migrate to the same area. Previously, the Five Points section of town was the center of grocery stores and markets. With Oakwood Market, Little Stores, and Cut-Rate opening in the area, this section of West Sullivan became known as Supermarket Row.

LITTLE STORE, 1960. When the Little Store opened on West Sullivan Street in January 1953, it was the first store in the region to have a complete bakery located inside a grocery store. The bakery department featured decorated cakes and was one of the top departments in the store. The store was also the first in the area to have checkout counters with movable belts and in-and-out automatic doors.

CUT-RATE MARKET. Thomas LaGuardia Sr. came to Kingsport in the early 1930s and worked as a wholesale produce dealer. Falling in love with Kingsport, he and his family stayed and made Kingsport their home. In 1935, LaGuardia opened the Cut-Rate Market in Five Points. A few years later in 1940, a new location was built at 440 East Sullivan Street. Thomas LaGuardia Jr. and Henry T. Helton became owners of the company, and by 1959, the name changed to Giant. Giant became a successful, locally owned grocery store chain. Below, Cut-Rate's frozen food department was one of the largest in Kingsport. This 1949 image shows an unidentified employee offering samples of Minute Maid orange juice.

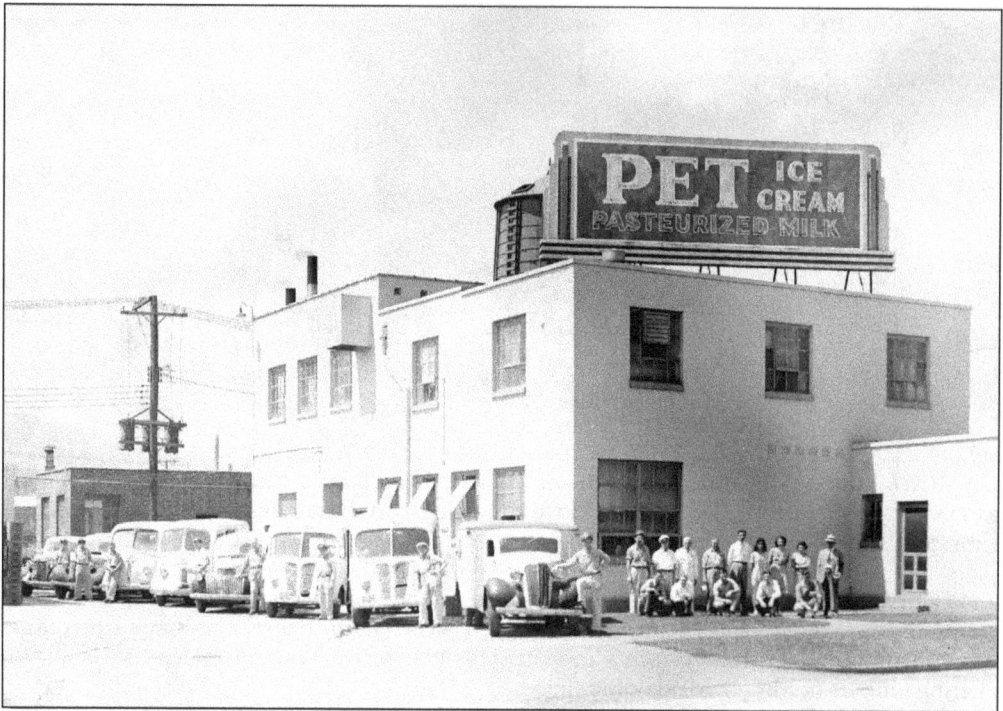

PET DAIRY PRODUCTS. PET Dairy Products began operations in Kingsport in 1930. This undated photograph shows the PET dairy plant on the corner of Clay and Market Streets. PET sold milk, buttermilk, chocolate milk, cream, cheese, and ice cream. The company was one of the main suppliers of dairy products to local businesses. The plant moved to Konnarock Road in 1955 and ceased operations in Kingsport in 2009.

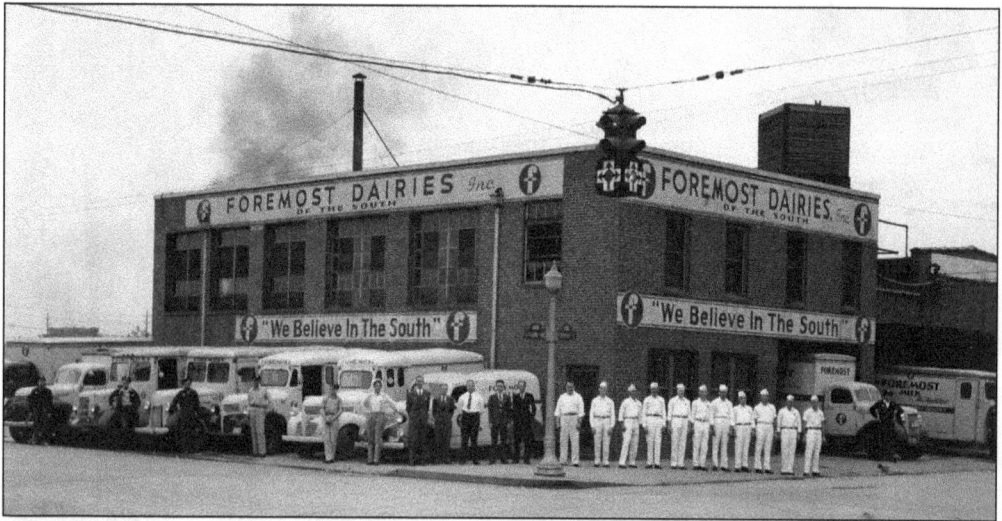

FOREMOST DAIRIES, 1946. Foremost Dairies opened in 1943. The company was located on the corner of Market and Cherokee Streets in a building formerly occupied by City Creamery. In 1968, the name was changed to Farmbest and operations were moved to Bristol. Like PET Dairy Products, Foremost produced and sold milk, cream, ice cream, and a variety of other dairy products.

OWL MARKET, 1951. The Owl Market celebrated its grand opening in May 1951. Located at 508 East Center Street, the store was owned by Jason Jenkins and Raul N. McClain. The store was marketed as the grocery store without a door and the store that never closed. The market was located between Nard's Sport Shop and Kingsport Tire Recapping Company. Customers could buy a variety of groceries, newspapers, magazines, and toiletries.

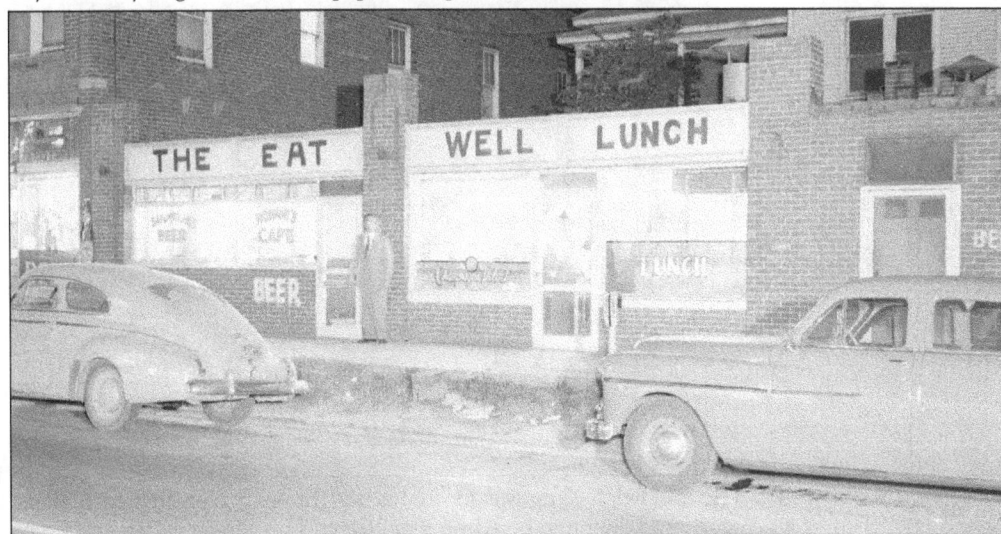

EAT WELL LUNCH, 1950. The Eat Well Lunch was operated by David Solomon. An immigrant from Lebanon, Solomon came to Kingsport in 1945. The restaurant was located at 335–337 East Sullivan Street. David Solomon was also the proprietor of Dave's Fruit and News.

HANEY'S, 1938. Haney's Place, owned by Salman and Della Haney, was located at 405 Cherokee Street. Haney's Place began operating in Kingsport around 1922. Shortly after Salman's death in 1942, Haney's Place became the site of another restaurant called the Victory Lunch.

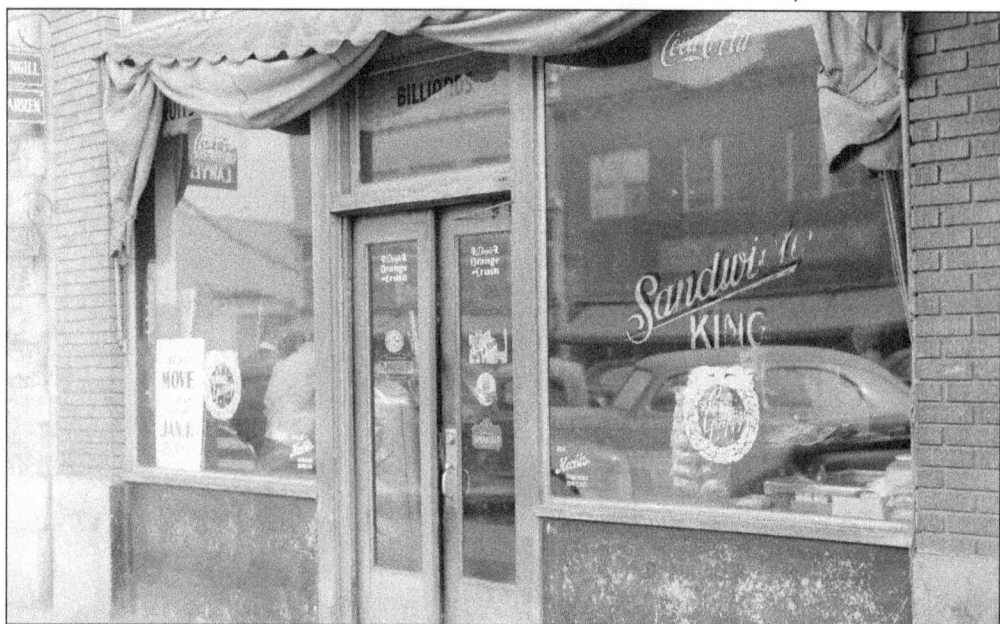

SANDWICH KING, 1946. The Sandwich King was located at 207 Broad Street next to Wallace News. The business was owned and operated by Anna Mae Richardson Sharp. It was started by Anna and her first husband, W.L. Richardson, around 1939. After his death, she continued to run the business. In 1947, the Sandwich King moved to Main Street, and the building was remodeled and became home to Betty Gay.

HANDY'S RESTAURANT, 1949. James Mead, operator of Handy's Restaurant, poses in front of the restaurant at 418 Cherokee Street. The restaurant, owned by J. Mack Ray, was located in the Five Points section of town. Pictured below are James Mead (far right) and unidentified employees behind the counter at Handy's.

CENTER STREET GRILL, 1947. The Center Street Grill formally opened on March 17, 1946. The restaurant was located at 504 West Center Street in the building formerly occupied by Major's Drive-In. The Center Street Grill was owned by Drushal "Happy" and Cardwell Hounchell. Happy was a popular Kingsport businessman and barber. He had several businesses, including the Model City Barber Shop, Five Points Barber Shop, Joyland Cottages, and Beauty Rest Grill.

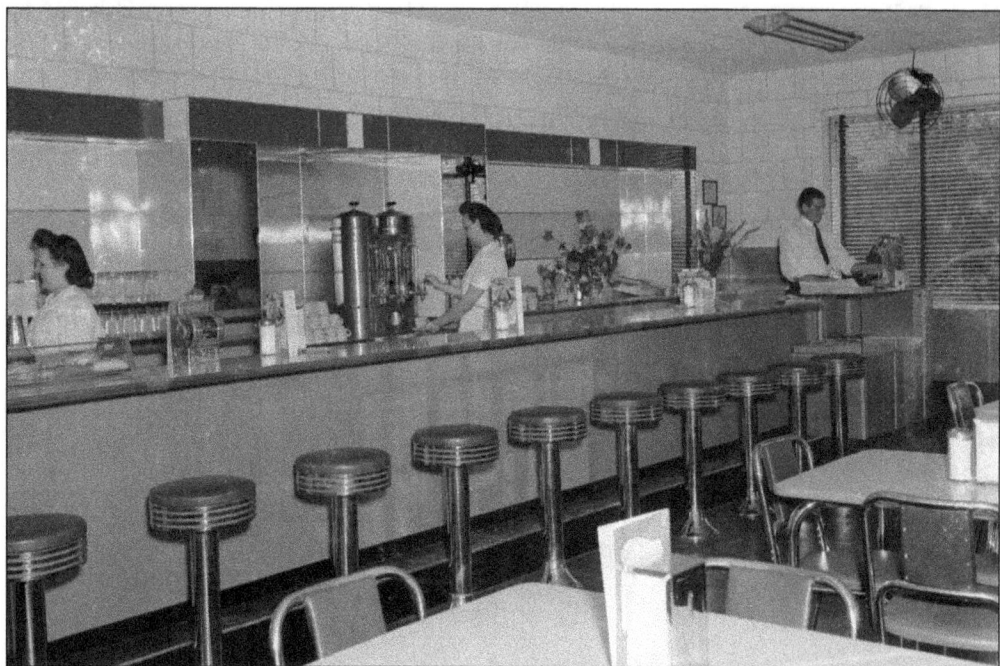

CENTER STREET GRILL INTERIOR, 1947. The Center Street Grill specialized in Southern home-cooked meals. When it first opened, the establishment's hours were 5 a.m. to 12 a.m. The restaurant's proximity to the Kingsport Press and other Kingsport industries made it a popular eating place for downtown workers.

CENTER STREET RESTAURANT, 1956. The Center Street Grill had a major renovation in the 1950s, and its name changed to Center Street Restaurant. The restaurant was managed by Cardwell and Alberta Hounchell. Jack May, owner of Jack's Grill in Sullivan Gardens, took ownership of the restaurant and continued to run the business for many years. May also managed the Little Store Luncheonette.

MACK RAY CAFETERIA, 1959. J. Mack Ray was a successful restaurateur in Kingsport who owned Handy's Restaurant and Mack Ray Cafeteria. Ray came to Kingsport from Newport, where he once served as vice mayor. Ray opened the Mack Ray Cafeteria on East Market Street in 1943. The business featured a cafeteria and luncheonette. In 1956, the restaurant moved to Commerce Street. Ray served as a Democratic senator in the 1960s.

TALLY HO, 1951. The Tally Ho was located at 502 East Center Street in the former home of the Chicken Hut. Tally Ho was owned by Elizabeth "Libby" and Wallace McDannel. The restaurant's specialty was fried chicken and steaks. The Tally Ho was the first restaurant in Kingsport to serve swordfish steaks.

UNITED NATIONS RESTAURANT, 1945. The United Nations Restaurant was located at 209 East New Street and was managed by Lucia E. Klein (third from left). Klein came to Kingsport from Washington, DC, and opened the restaurant on July 4, 1945. Rose Marie McKamey, a pianist and vocalist, was a featured entertainer at the restaurant. In 1946, the business was sold to Joseph E. Gill and Felix G. McMillion, who opened the Macgil Restaurant.

90

TEXAS STEER, 1950. The Texas Steer Drive-In was located at 420 West Center Street and was originally owned by Bill Harrell. The Texas Steer opened for business in 1950. It advertised many specialties, including Texas Steer Sandwiches, grilled hot dogs, barbecue, and the Steerburger. The restaurant also became known for its take-out fried chicken business. Customers could eat inside, have dinner at the curb, order take-out, or make delivery orders.

TEXAS STEER STAFF. This 1955 photograph shows the Texas Steer staff posing for the camera. Pictured from left to right are Jim Williams, Helen McReynolds, ? Owens, Patty Colley, Betty Winston, Jean Ball, Shirley Tate, Helen Sullivan, Sue Adkins, and Jerry Brooks. Guy Williams became owner of the business around 1953. The Texas Steer was a popular place for local teenagers to visit at night.

BEACON DRIVE-IN, 1953. The Beacon Drive-In was located at 503 West Center Street and held its grand opening in January 1954. More than 2,000 guests were treated to barbecued ham, coleslaw, and hush puppies that were cooked in the barbecue pit. The Beacon boasted the most modern and largest barbecue pit in the south. The restaurant was owned by Bill Harrell, the original owner of the Texas Steer. William P. and Martha Majors purchased the restaurant in 1955.

PAL'S, 1956. In 1956, the first Pal's Sudden Service, founded by Fred "Pal" Barger, opened in Downtown Kingsport at 327 Revere Street. The original menu consisted of milk shakes, soft drinks, "frenchie fries," and "sauceburgers." Pal's was the first restaurant to win the Malcolm Baldrige National Quality Award and has been awarded the Tennessee Excellence Award twice. Today, there are more than 20 locations in East Tennessee and Southwest Virginia.

Seven

TRANSPORTATION

CLAYTON TRANSPORTATION COMPANY. This undated photograph shows a taxi owned by the Clayton Transportation Company. The company was located on Main Street and was owned by J.M. Clayton and C.J. Johnson. The company ceased operations in 1927.

ALLEN'S GARAGE, 1920. Allen's Garage, owned by W. Arthur Allen, opened in January 1923. Located on Shelby Street, the garage operated as a service station and automobile repair shop. For a few months in 1924, the garage was owned by W.A. Dishner and was named Dishner Motor Company. The company was repurchased by Allen, and Allen's Garage eventually became part of W.A. Allen Motors, Inc.

FAIN MOTOR COMPANY. The Fain Motor Company, successor of the Kingsport Garage, began operating on November 1, 1920. Kingsport Garage had operated at this location on Sullivan Street since 1918. The Fain Motor Company was the largest garage in Sullivan County at one time. The company was managed by James R. Fain, and W. Arthur Allen served as secretary.

MIDGET CAR, 1945. The Hummingbird—a tiny, maroon-colored convertible—was created by Talmadge Judd in 1945. Judd, who is seated in the car, built the midget convertible in his backyard workshop. He was the owner of Judd's Lockshop and was known as "Kingsport's Mr. Fix-It." The car attracted worldwide fame after it was featured in *Popular Mechanics*. The Hummingbird could run 50 miles per gallon and weighed 1,350 pounds. It was featured at many county fairs around the region.

WHIZZER MOTORBIKE. Unidentified men look at the Whizzer Motorbike in this 1947 image. The photograph was taken inside the Sport Shop, which was Kingsport's exclusive dealer of Whizzer Motorbikes. In 1939, Whizzer Motorbikes were first produced by Breene-Taylor Engineering, a manufacturer of airplane parts in Los Angeles.

City Bus Terminal, 1948. The City Bus Terminal, located on the corner of Main and Commerce Streets, opened in 1943. The terminal was operated by the City Transportation Company. The company had previously operated out of a terminal at 104 East Main Street. The City Transportation Company was granted the exclusive right to operate streetcars and buses by the City of Kingsport in the 1920s. The company was started by Roy Seals.

Bus Terminal, 1946. This photograph shows the Union Bus Terminal on Cherokee Street, which opened around 1942. Managed by Ralph J. Sproles, the property was owned by W. Arthur Allen, and the terminal was designed by Allen Dryden Sr. The terminal building at the right of the photograph housed apartments, the Kingsport Bowling Center, and the Cherokee Grill. Today, the terminal building is known as the W.A. Allen Building.

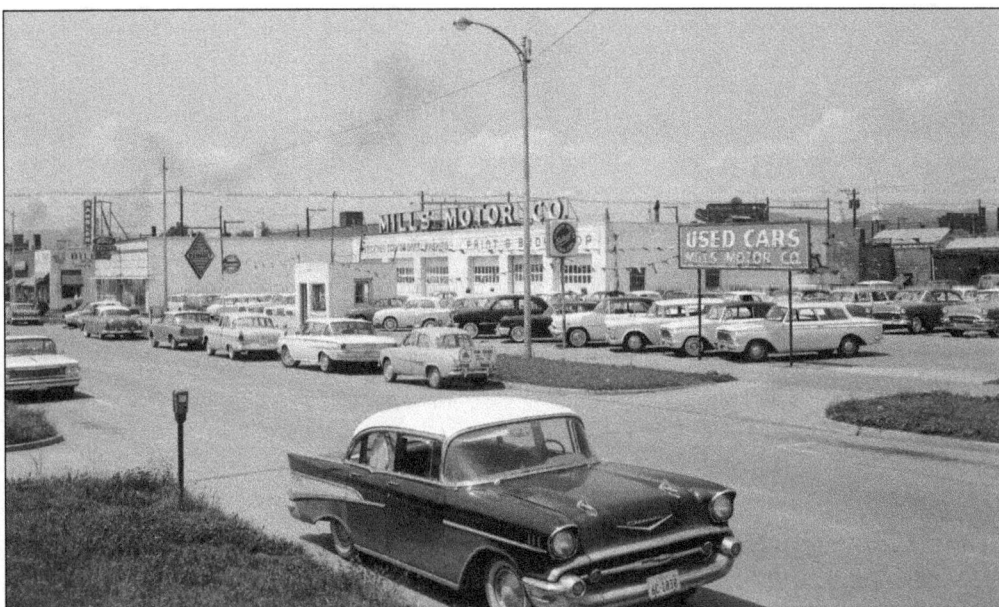

MILLS MOTOR COMPANY, 1962. The Mills Motor Company opened in the Kenner Building, located at Shelby and Market Streets, in 1925. The company was managed by William H. Mills with assistance from W.A. Dishner. The company started as a dealer of new and used Fords and later sold Chrysler, Renault, and Rambler. Harry R. Mills was president of the company when this photograph was taken in 1962.

STUDEBAKER, 1946. A large crowd gathers around a 1947 Studebaker that was being given away in a raffle. The giveaway was part of a fundraising effort to build a Teen Center. Construction on the Teen Center, which was located on Cumberland Street, began in 1947. Studebakers were sold in Kingsport by Brashear Motors on the corner of Oak Street and Bristol Highway.

MORELOCK MOTORS. Rass Morelock came to Kingsport in 1937 and worked for Craft Motors and Brashear Motors. He opened his own business, Morelock Motors, with two employees in 1943. Morelock sold Nash automobiles and used cars. In 1947, he was awarded the honor of being the first Nash dealer in the area and qualified under the Nash 10-point dealer program. The 1947 photograph above shows the exterior of Morelock Motors, which was located at 835 Bristol Highway. The 1956 photograph below shows the sales room and the Morelock Luncheonette. The luncheonette served breakfast items, hamburgers, hot dogs, fountain drinks, sandwiches, and steaks.

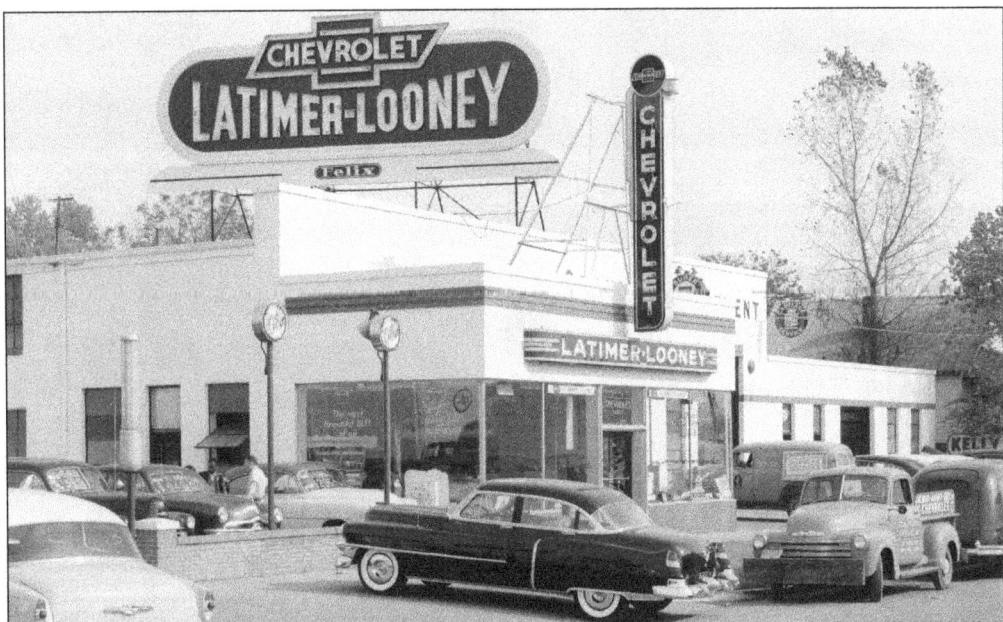

LATIMER-LOONEY, 1953. The Chevrolet Latimer-Looney dealership opened for business in 1938 and was the successor to the W.A. Allen Chevrolet Company. The Chevrolet dealership was founded by J.L. "Lane" Latimer and R.F. "Bob" Looney. Looney later bought out Latimer and continued to run the company with his sons Alex and Bob Jr. The building in this photograph was located at 707 East Sullivan Street.

HOLSTON AUTO SUPPLY. Holston Auto Supply was located at 321 West Market Street. When this photograph was taken in 1952, J. Matthew Nelson was the president and general manager of the company. Holston Auto Supply opened in Kingsport with only two employees, Nelson and J.H. Rogers, in February 1946. By 1952, the company expanded to a second location in Rogersville and had more than 30 employees.

TRI-CITY MOTORS, 1957. Tri-City Motors, located on West Center Street, was a Desoto and Plymouth automobile dealer. The Tri-City Motors building also housed the LeMoyne System Auto Painters, which was the first production and automobile paint shop in the area. Tri-City Motors was the successor of the Wallin Motor Company. Tri-City Motors opened in 1953.

SEALS. The Seals Motor Corporation seen in this 1950 photograph was located at 118 Shelby Street. A year later, Seals moved to Market Street. Seals Motor Corporation was opened by Tyler G. Seals in 1945. The company specialized in sales of Hudson automobiles and automobile repair.

CRAFT MOTORS. The Tennessee Motor Company—exclusive Ford agents—first started in February 1924 and opened on Shelby and Market Streets. In 1925, the business moved to Sullivan Street, where it was managed by R.C. Good. In 1935, Ryland G. Craft and E.B. Tidwell took ownership of the Tennessee Motor Company. The name was changed to Craft Motors in 1936. Craft Motors was located on the corner of East Sullivan and Commerce Streets. Ryland G. Craft was a well-known, politically active businessman from Gate City, Virginia. Craft was the owner of Gate City Motor Company and served as a senator in Virginia. Below, the 1950 models of Fords are on display in the Craft Motors showroom in this 1949 photograph.

TOM YANCEY, INC., 1951. Tom Yancey sold Lincoln and Mercury automobiles. He opened for business in the back of Thomason Esso Station in 1948. Yancey moved his company to this building on Revere Street in October 1948. During construction, the roof collapsed and killed four people, injuring 12. It was one of the worst building accidents in Kingsport's history.

YOU AUTO BUY NOW, 1958. The You Auto Buy Now campaign, a national effort to combat the declining sales of automobiles, brought virtually every automobile dealership in Kingsport to downtown. Dealerships set up automobiles for display along Broad Street. Cherokee Motors displayed its stock of automobiles on the 200 block of Broad Street in front of Fuller and Hillman, Nettie Lee, and Freels.

CHEROKEE MOTORS. Cherokee Motors first opened for business in December 1937. Originally located on Cherokee Street, the company had several locations downtown throughout its history. Pictured above is Cherokee Motors in 1959, when it was located at 600 East Sullivan Street. James A. Clark was the president of Cherokee Motors. The business sold Buick, Oldsmobile, and GMC trucks. The 1950 photograph below shows the parts and accessories counter located inside Cherokee Motors.

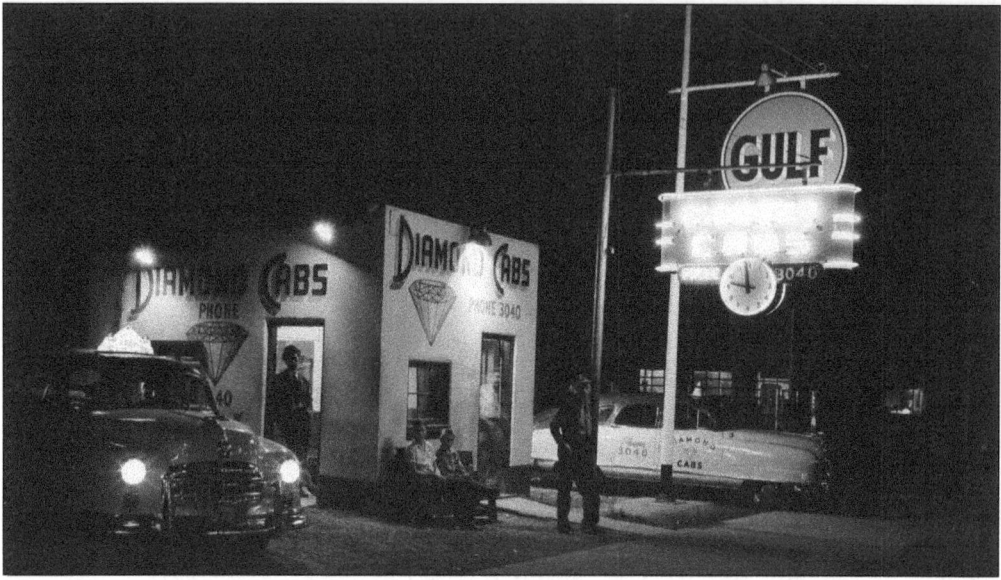

DIAMOND CABS, 1950. Owned by Rass Morelock from Morelock Motors, Diamond Cabs operated a fleet of 16 Nash Airflyte four-door sedans. The transportation company began in 1950 as a consolidation of the Plymouth and Charles Cab Companies. Diamond Cabs was located at 309 Cherokee Street.

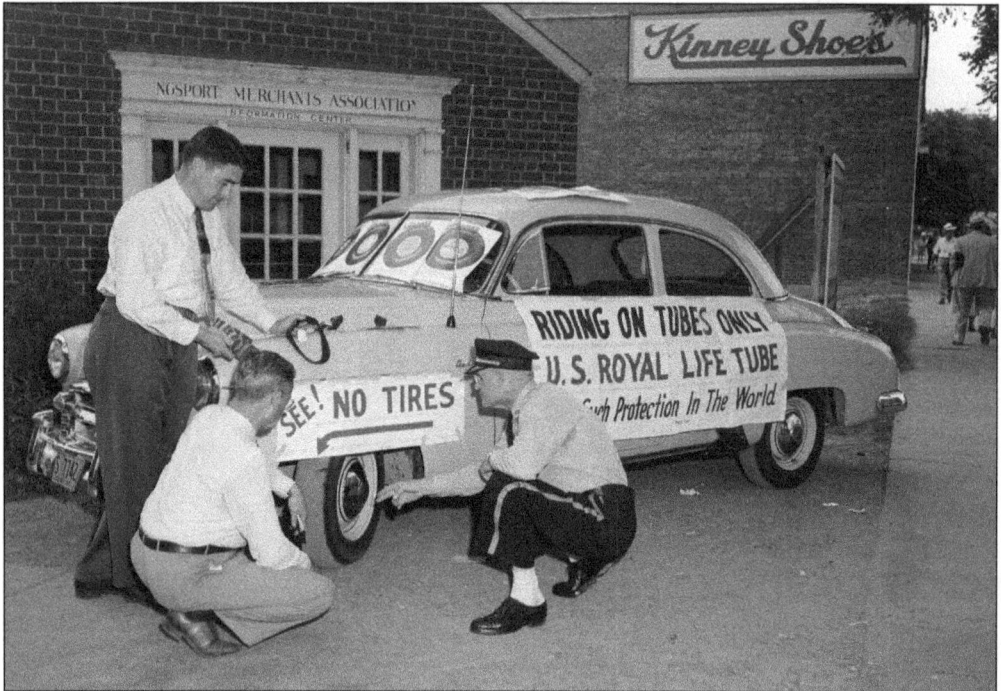

US ROYAL LIFE TUBES, 1950. This car, seen parked in front of the chamber of commerce on Broad Street, was brought to town to demonstrate the new US Royal Nylon Life Tube. The tubes were advertised as providing better driving and riding safety. Dave Latham (left), from the US Rubber Company, examines the vehicle with G.T. McGuire, owner of a Kingsport tire company, and George W. Fletcher, Kingsport's chief of police.

DUFFER-TAYLOR, 1950. Duffer-Taylor Tire Service operated as a service station, tire dealer, and repair shop. The business, previously called Young's Tires, was located at 200 West Center Street. Duffer-Taylor was owned by A. Frank Taylor and Morton H. Duffer, former vice mayor and alderman. Taylor was part of the *Frank and Mack Show*, a comedy and variety act with partner Mack Riddle. Duffer and Taylor opened the business in 1947.

KITE'S ESSO SERVICENTER, 1948. Kite's Esso Servicenter was located on the corner of East Center and Cherokee Streets. Owned by Ula Kite, the building was also home to A.K. Motor Sales and the Kingsport Radiator Shop. The company sold automobile accessories, supplies, and used cars.

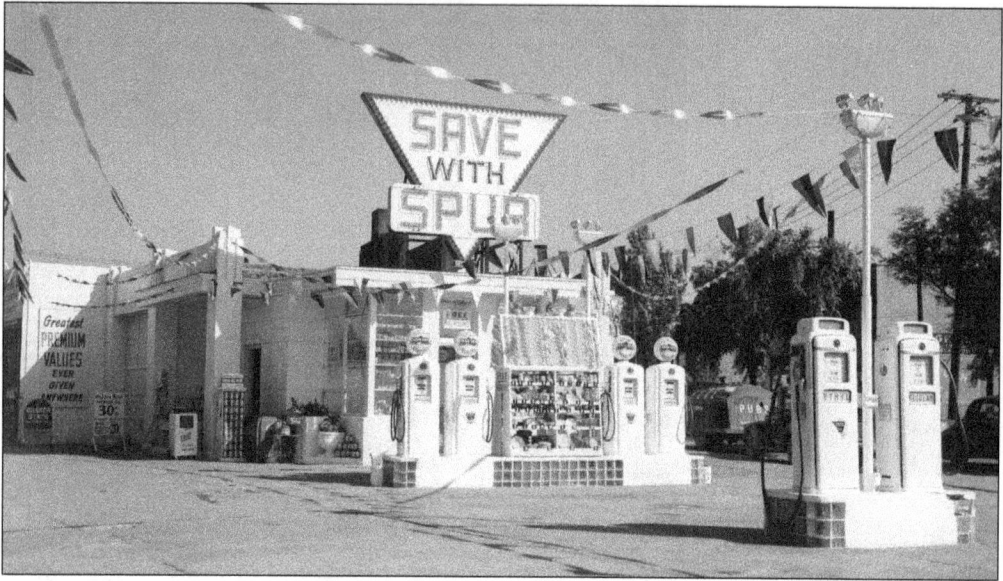

SAVE WITH SPUR. The Spur Station opened on the corner of East Center and Sullivan Streets in May 1951. The service station advertised low prices and high-quality gas. It was conveniently located in the downtown business district. The opening weekend of the station was celebrated with balloons, prizes, and free gifts. The company imported orchids from Hawaii to give out to women attending the celebration. The grand prize being given away was an Admiral Triple-Play Radio and Phonograph Combination. The 1951 photograph above shows the exterior of the Spur Station. In the 1952 photograph below, employees of the Spur Station pose in front of the gas pumps and a display of dinnerware.

Eight

DOWNTOWN
STREET SCENES

VIEW DOWN BROAD, 1946. This view down Broad Street was taken several years after the medians and parkways were removed. The Broad Street Project that began around 1938 increased the traffic lanes, extended the sidewalks, and allowed angle parking on the street. Broad Street has been reconfigured once again and features smaller traffic lanes with angle parking in the middle of the street.

200 Block of Broad, 1946. Taken from the corner of Broad and Market Streets, this view shows the west side of the 200 block of Broad Street. Businesses on this block included the Charles Store Company, Woolworth's, W.T. Grant, and S.H. Kress.

J. Fred Johnson and Company, 1946. J. Fred Johnson and Company, previously located at Shelby and Main Streets, moved to 144–146 Broad Street in the 1930s. The Palace Fruit and News and Palace Barber Shop were located next door. Palace was opened by Paul Nottingham and John Tranbarger in 1925 and closed in 1966.

BROAD AND CENTER STREET, 1946. This 1946 photograph shows the east side of the 200 block of Broad Street, which was home to Freels, Sobel's, Nettie Lee, Morgan's Shoes, and Fuller and Hillman. The Freels building has undergone a renovation in recent years, exposing the building's original facade seen here.

CORNER OF BROAD AND MARKET. This 1946 photograph shows a crowd gathering in front of the State Theatre, which was located at the 100 block of Broad Street. Signs on the theater's marquee advertised that admission was 30¢ plus 6¢ for a war tax. Next door to the theater was the J.C. Penney Company, which moved to a new building on Broad Street in 1949.

GRADUATES' DAY ORGANIZERS, 1941. Organizers of Graduates' Day pose for a photograph on Broad Street. Graduates' Day was started as a celebration for Kingsport's high school graduates and was sponsored by the Kingsport Merchants Association. The first Graduates' Day was held on May 14, 1940. Pictured from left to right are Dr. Will Hutchins, Sam Bingham, Vernon Miller, Hugh Nelms, and Jim Beasley.

PARADE. The Dobyns-Bennett High School band marches down Broad Street during this 1946 parade. The Dobyns-Bennett High School band and other students used to march through the streets of downtown on Friday nights before football games.

AMERICAN LEGION CARNIVAL, 1950. The first American Legion Carnival in Kingsport was held October 14–19, 1929. The carnivals were sponsored by the American Legion, Hammond Post No. 3. They took place in the fall until 1936, when they became a summer affair. The carnivals were held in various locations downtown for decades.

WAITING FOR SANTA, 1948. A large crowd has converged downtown for the annual Christmas parade and for a glimpse of Santa. The Downtown Kingsport Christmas parade begins with the arrival of Santa on the Santa Train. This picture, taken around the intersection of Broad and Center Streets, shows Broad Street decorated with festive garlands.

VIEW DOWN BROAD, 1958. This view down Broad Street was taken during the You Auto Buy Now campaign. More than 350 automobiles from dealerships around the city lined the streets of downtown. The campaign became a city-wide effort that inspired other retail merchants. Merchants around the city began using the Kingsport Value Carnival theme to coincide with the automobile campaign and to increase sales across the city.

EAST CENTER AND BROAD, 1949. This 1949 photograph was taken from the intersection of Broad and Center Streets. Pedestrians are seen waiting to cross Broad Street. Pedestrian walking lights were not put at intersections downtown until 1977.

1946. This 1946 photograph shows Wallace News, one of the longest-running establishments located in Downtown Kingsport. Wallace News shared a marquee and building with the Baby Shop. The Baby Shop was owned by Harvey and Florence Penyon. Other businesses in this image include Sterchi Brothers Furniture, Sullivan County Bank, Sandwich King Restaurant, and Western Union.

MARKET AND BROAD STREETS. This 1955 photograph shows businesses on Broad Street as well as a view down Market Street. The Carlton Shop, located on the corner of Broad and Market, carried women's clothing and was managed by Jackie S. Bacon. The billboard on top of the building was for the J.T. Parker Insurance Company located on Market Street.

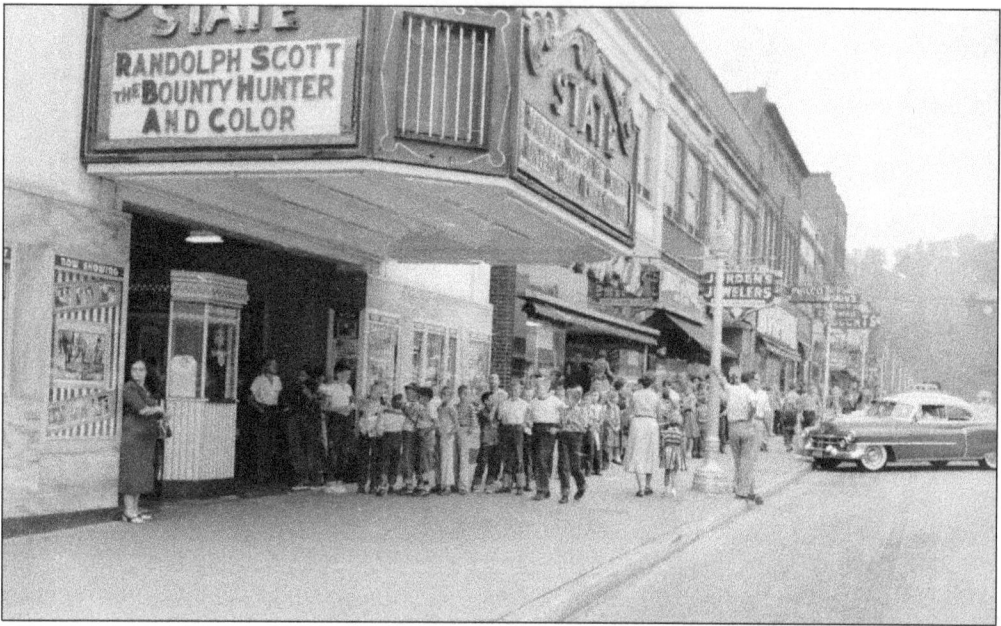

IN LINE AT THE STATE. The State Theatre was a popular place to be when this photograph was taken in 1954. Children of all ages are lined up on the sidewalks in front of the theater and surrounding businesses. The theater was showing *The Bounty Hunter*, starring Randolph Scott.

ADVANCE. Advance, a home and automobile supply store, was located on Broad Street between the Darling Shop and Moskin's. Advance opened in 1956, around the time this photograph was taken. The new store featured a new facade and a remodel of the interior. Moskin's Credit Clothing was located at 137 Broad Street in the Strauss Building.

FIRST NATIONAL BANK, 1946. The First National Bank building, located on the corner of Center and Broad Streets, was built in the 1920s. The bank building housed a variety of offices for many years. Next door to the bank was Montgomery Ward, located in the building now known as the Progress Building. The Elite Beauty Salon and Parks-Belk were also located on this block of Broad Street.

J. FRED JOHNSON AND COMPANY, 1962. J. Fred Johnson and Company moved into the building at the corner of Broad and Center Streets in 1956, the same year it celebrated its 50th anniversary. The new, million-dollar building had the first escalator in upper East Tennessee. In 1954, the company was purchased by Lovemans, Inc., of Chattanooga, but the store continued to operate under the name of J. Fred Johnson.

BROADSTREET FURNITURE. In 1963, Broadstreet Furniture underwent a significant remodel of its interior and exterior. Among the changes to the exterior was the new facade seen in this image. The company's motto was "Where good furniture is not expensive." Broadstreet Furniture, opened by George W. Taylor and S. Flem Dobyns in 1944, was located between the Strand Theatre and Palace Fruit and News.

SOUTHERN SHOE STORE, 1951. Southern Shoe Store was located at 119 Broad Street. The company opened in November 1935 and advertised a selection of more than 5,000 pairs of shoes.

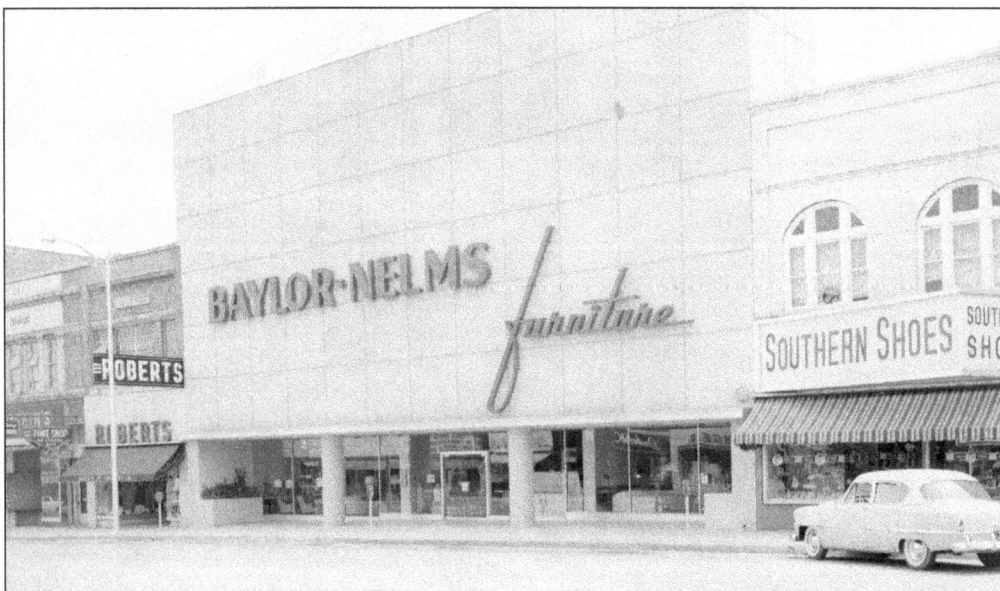

BAYLOR-NELMS, 1957. Baylor-Nelms Furniture was located at 125 Broad Street. B.H. Baylor and James E. Nelms purchased the Johnson–Van Trease Furniture Company in 1929 and established the Baylor-Nelms Furniture Company. Baylor had previously owned and managed the Baylor Furniture Company, and Nelms was a former postmaster and local businessman. The building's facade, seen in this image, has been removed, and in recent years, the Baylor-Nelms building has undergone an extensive restoration project.

MAIN STREET. This 1950 photograph shows shops on Main Street, including Watson's, American Shoe Shop, Brown Derby, and the Double Eagle Billiard Parlor. On the second floor, above Watson's, was the Independent Order of Odd Fellows Hall (IOOF), which was a meeting place for the Lovedale Lodge of IOOF and other fraternal organizations.

WEST MAIN STREET, 1946. The Army Store, located at 136 West Main Street, was established by B.A. Bowers of Knoxville in 1918. The Foster Auto Supply Company was located at 132 West Main Street and was originally owned by Lewis Foster. The company was purchased by Fayne Bell and Carl Burton in 1957. Star Lunch, at the far right of the image, was operated by Thomas and Nickalos Kastsinas.

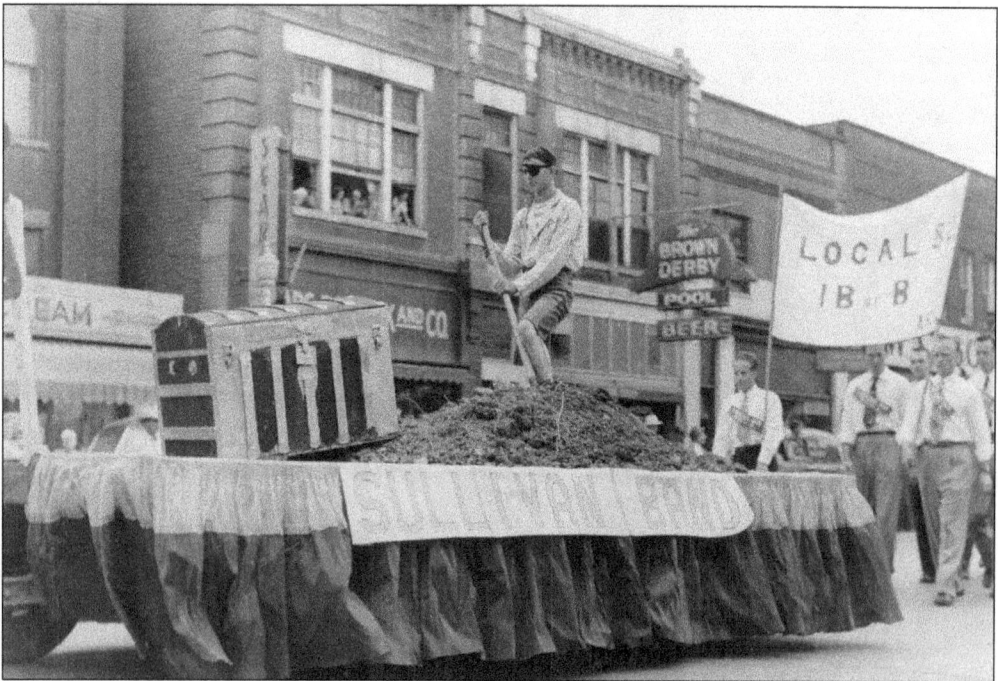

PARADE ON EAST MAIN STREET. A parade float for the Sullivan Band makes its way down East Main Street in this undated photograph. Behind the float are members of the International Brotherhood of Bookbinders Local 82 union from the Kingsport Press.

Bon Ton Cleaners, 1946. Bon Ton Cleaners opened on Commerce Street in 1935. Neal Ketron, owner and manager of the store, reopened the business at this 115 East Market Street location in 1945. Other businesses in this image include the Sport Shop and Billings Grocery. Billings Grocery was owned by Dewey C. Billings.

East Market, 1946. The 100 block of East Market Street was home to the Harkleroad Feed Company, Weaver's Shoe Shop, Weaver Apartments, and Anderson Furniture Company. Weaver's Shoe Shop, owned by Ernest A. Weaver, was located at 118 East Market. Weaver Apartments were located at 116 1/2 East Market Street. The apartments were located on the second floor of the building.

CHEROKEE STREET. This 1950 photograph shows a view down the 200 block of Cherokee Street. Businesses on this block included the Star Shoe Shop, the Kingsport Camera Shop, and Radio Electric Supply. The Star Shoe Shop at 206 Cherokee Street was opened in 1925 by C.E. Brown.

EAST MARKET AND CHEROKEE. The intersection of East Market and Cherokee Streets was the scene of a traffic accident in this 1961 photograph. Anderson Furniture (left) was owned by Charles Anderson and opened for business in 1945. The Busy Bee Lunch (right) opened in 1930 and was owned and operated by Nick Karamblockis. The popular restaurant closed in 1963.

SOBEL'S, 1956. Sobel's opened in this location on the corner of Center and Commerce Streets in 1948. It closed for business in 2000. The dental offices of Dr. W.P. Johnson and Dr. R.H. Montgomery were located on the top floor of the Sobel's building. The medical offices were accessible from Commerce Street.

CENTER AND BROAD STREET, 1956. This view of the intersection of Broad and Center Streets was taken in 1956. The First National Bank Building on the corner has been renovated in recent years and is still one of the most recognizable buildings in Downtown Kingsport. Other businesses in the image include Holston Drug on Center Street and Montgomery Ward, Parks-Belk, and Elite Beauty Salon on Broad Street.

EAST SULLIVAN STREET, 1946. This image of East Sullivan Street was taken from the intersection of Cherokee Street in Five Points. Charles Restaurant, on the corner, was originally owned by Charles Joseph and Salim Massoud. Later owners of the restaurant were Ollie Shadeed and Chris Martin. The Ben Franklin Store, which opened in 1941, featured fountain service and a luncheonette.

FIVE POINTS. This 1946 photograph shows an area that has long been referred to as Five Points. Five Points was once one of the busiest sections in downtown. The area had a large concentration of markets, grocery stores, and restaurants. The streets associated with Five Points were Sullivan, Cherokee, Charlemont, and Boone.

EAST MARKET STREET. The Times-News Building was located on the 200 block of East Market Street. The *Kingsport Times-News*, the first newspaper in Kingsport, was purchased by C.P. Edwards Jr. and a group of stockholders in 1938. This photograph of the building was taken in 1946. Since 1970, the *Times-News* offices have been located on Lynn Garden Drive.

CHEROKEE STREET, 1950. This 1950 photograph shows a view of businesses along Cherokee Street near the intersection of East Market Street. Businesses in this image include Dorton Motor Sales, Star Shoe Shop, Kingsport Camera Shop, the Busy Bee Restaurant, Rogers & Fuller Realtors, J&M Furniture Company, and Radio Electric Supply Company.

FIVE POINTS, 1953. The Western Auto Associate Store was located on the corner of Charlemont and Sullivan Streets. The store opened at this location in September 1952 and was owned by Pete Ramsey. The shop offered items for the car, home, and farm as well as items for recreation, including appliances, toys, radios, housewares, paint, and hardware. Other businesses in the photograph include United Furniture and Pete Moore's.

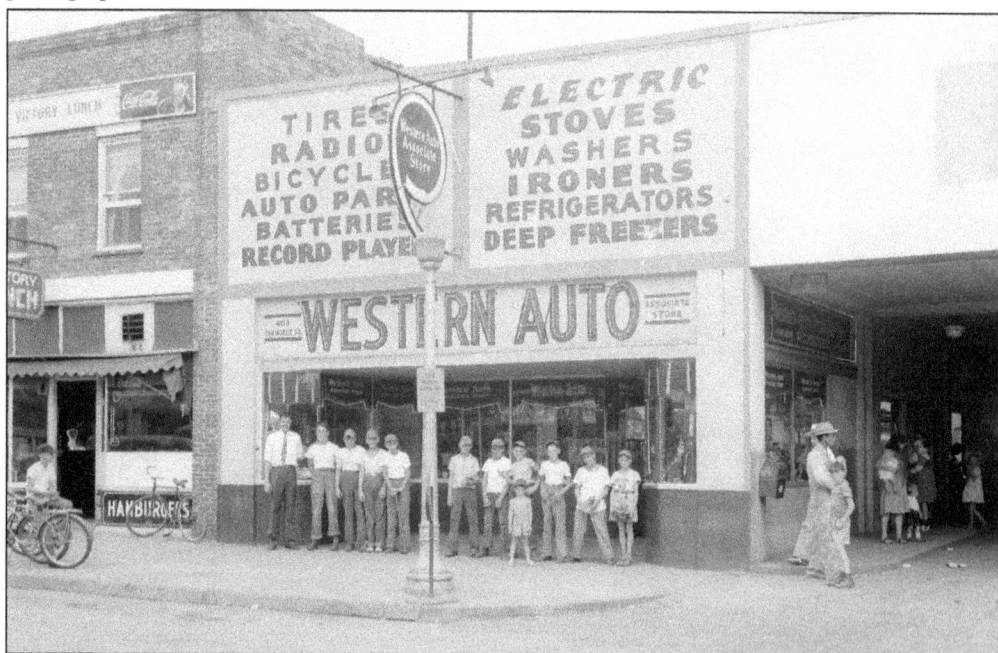

CHEROKEE STREET, 1946. Frank Medearis opened the Western Auto Associate Store on Cherokee Street in 1936. A few years after this photograph was taken, Medearis opened Medearis Auto Supply at this same location. Western Auto was located between the Union Bus Terminal and Victory Lunch. Victory Lunch was located at 405 Cherokee Street and was owned by Sam Williams.

EAST SULLIVAN STREET, 1951. The City Mission was founded by Thomas A. Williams in 1936. The City Mission provided meals, lodging, and assistance to people in need. Williams came to Kingsport in 1917 and operated the Magic City Barber Shop for several years. After his death in 1967, his wife, Clara, continued to run the City Mission. The City Mission held church services every day and often featured visiting pastors.

DOWNTOWNER, 1962. The Downtowner Motor Inn was located on the corner of West Center and Shelby Streets in Downtown Kingsport. The Downtowner opened in 1960 with 104 rooms. In 1974, the facility was called the Port O' Kings Motor Inn and Restaurant. In 1981, the motel was known as the Travelers Lodge. Attorney Bobby Tate bought the building during the 1980s and renamed it the Kingsport Inn. It was demolished in the early 1990s.

BROAD STREET. This view of Broad Street was captured in 1968. Taken from the middle of the street, Broad Street is seen anchored by the Clinchfield Railroad Station on Main Street. When this image was taken, Broad Street was still the main commercial district in Kingsport. As with most downtowns, the scenery began to change as businesses migrated out of downtown to shopping malls and previously outlying areas.

ABOUT THE ARCHIVES

The Archives of the City of Kingsport collects, preserves, houses, and makes accessible many records pertaining to the City of Kingsport. The archives collects documents, photographs, journals, scrapbooks, business and organizational records, and correspondence to preserve the documentary heritage of Kingsport and its inhabitants. The Friends of the Archives (FOA) is a nonprofit support group that aids in promoting the interests of the Archives of the City of Kingsport. The FOA provides volunteer resources and outreach programs and raises funds to supplement the needs and resources of the archives.

BIBLIOGRAPHY

Brockman, Jim, Bill King, and Jane Shivell. *Local History: A Scrapbook on Kingsport Prepared for American History, Dobyns-Bennett High School.* 1942.

Egan, Martha Avaleen. "Kingsport Press." *Tennessee Encyclopedia of History and Culture.* Carroll Van West, ed. Knoxville: Tennessee Historical Society and Rutledge Hill Press, 1998.

Egan, Martha Avaleen and Nellie McNeil. Images of America: *Kingsport.* Charleston, SC: Arcadia Publishing, 1998.

Gaines, Eula Lee. *History of City of Kingsport and Bloomingdale Area.* N.D.

Kingsport: City of Industries, Schools, Churches and Homes. Kingsport, TN: Rotary Club, 1937.

Kingsport Times News archives, 1916–1977.

Long, Howard. *Kingsport: A Romance of Industry.* Kingsport, TN: The Sevier Press, 1928.

Porter, Dena Williams. *Sullivan County, Tennessee.* Johnson City, TN: Overmountain Press, 2003.

Wolfe, Margaret Ripley. *Kingsport, Tennessee: A Planned American City.* Lexington, KY: University Press of Kentucky, 1987.

Visit us at
arcadiapublishing.com

www.ingramcontent.com/pod-product-compliance
Lightning Source LLC
Chambersburg PA
CBHW080621110426
42813CB00006B/1571